For Natalie &
with love

For Natalie & Gene
with love

For Natalie & Gene
with love

For Natalie & Gene
with love

For Natalie & Gene
with love

For Natalie Gene
with love

For Natalie & Gene
with love
& love LOU

Louis Solomon

Louis Solomon, 70, television writer-producer and former screenwriter, died June 12 of cancer in Southold, Long Island.

Author of 10 books for young people, Solomon wrote the 1943 Broadway play, "Snafu" with Harold Buchman. Robert Benchley starred in the film version, which the dramatist wrote three years later, and Solomon contributed to the scenarios of two other pictures, "Mr. Winkle Goes To War" and "Mark Of The Renegade."

More recently, Solomon was coordinating producer of "The Great American Dream Machine" and wrote for other shows, including "Wide, Wide World."

He is survived by his widow, writer Wilma Shore, daughters Hilary Bendich and Dinah Stevenson, and three grandchildren.

6/19/81

THE
MA
&
PA
MURDERS AND
OTHER
PERFECT
CRIMES

Also by Louis Solomon

THE MA & PA MURDERS AND OTHER PERFECT CRIMES

BY LOUIS SOLOMON

J. B. LIPPINCOTT COMPANY / PHILADELPHIA AND NEW YORK

The photographs on the pages listed are reproduced here by permission of the following: The Bettmann Archive, Inc., 96; Courtesy of the Brooklyn Museum, 62, Bequest of A. Augustus Healy, 54; Brown Brothers, 32, 76, 81, 130, 132, 138, 141, 146, 153; United Press International, 15, 41, 46, 49, 104, 111, 113, 121, 125; Wide World Photos, 20, 23, 26, 31, 38.

U.S. Library of Congress Cataloging in Publication Data

Solomon, Louis, birth date
  The Ma & Pa murders and other perfect crimes.

  Published in 1976 by Scholastic Book Services under title: Great unsolved crimes.
    1. Crime and criminals—United States—Case studies—Juvenile literature. I. Title.
  HV6783.S55   1977   364.1′0973   76-56080
  ISBN-0-397-31577-5

For Viola

CONTENTS

THE
MA
&
PA
MURDERS AND
OTHER
PERFECT
CRIMES

THE GREAT FREE FALL FELONY:
The Hijacking of Northwest Airlines #305

•

UNTIL THE SOLITARY PASSENGER in the rear of Northwest Airlines Flight 305 handed stewardess Florence Shaffner a note, the transcontinental journey had been entirely routine. The liner was on the last leg—Portland, Ore. to Seattle, Wash.—of a five-stop run from Washington, D.C. What happened during that final hop made it a day to remember, not only for thirty-six passengers and six crew members, but for scores of frustrated FBI agents, an army of sheriff's deputies, volunteer manhunters, hound dogs, and the United States Army and Air Force.

The author of the note, who appeared on the passenger list as D. B. Cooper, free-fell into the heights of crime history as the only person ever to hijack a domestic airliner for profit without being caught or killed. Since that Thanksgiving eve, November 24, 1971, no other professional or amateur sky crook has successfully challenged his accomplishment.

Undoubtedly, D. B. had some special technical credentials which helped him fulfill his mission. Just how expert he was about floating in air became a matter of debate. One thing that couldn't be argued was his ability to make himself invisible, a not inconsiderable asset for any criminal enterprise. Indeed, he left so few traces of his venture that even the fellow travelers on his trip to nowhere could be forgiven for wondering whether he existed at all.

Of course, the record shows that a one-way passage for the twenty-five-minute flight from Portland to Seattle was bought by a man who gave his name as D. B. Cooper. But there was no reason for the ticket seller to remember him. To aircraft personnel on the ground or aloft, all passengers tend to look alike, unless they're complainers, or Jacqueline Onassis or Joe Namath or Henry Kissinger, or they don't observe the "No Smoking" and "Fasten Seat Belt" signs.

D. B. was not fussy or demanding. He made no impression on flight attendant Shaffner and her teammate Tina Mucklow when they welcomed him aboard. Even after he completed his trip, the best description that police prodding could produce from forty witnesses who had spent some three horrifying hours in his company was: "Kind of swarthy," "Sort of about fortyish," "About six feet tall." Somewhat more specific results of the police poll were that he had on a brown business suit and "he wore sunglasses." (The skyjacker's clothing turned out to be one of the most bewildering aspects of the caper.)

Artist's composite sketch of a man who called himself D. B. Cooper, based on witnesses' descriptions.

Oh, yes, add his carry-on luggage, the beat-up briefcase on his lap. It wasn't much help in identifying him, but without it, his note would have been ignored.

The fact that D. B. had chosen to sit by himself way back in the tail was not noteworthy until after he had made his move. Then it became apparent the seating arrangement was part of his plan. He was perched on the catbird seat. Like the outlaw in a Western movie saloon, his back was to the wall, nobody could surprise him from behind, and he could keep a commanding eye on what was happening.

Minutes after takeoff, when the "No Smoking" sign went off, D. B. made his debut. Flight attendant Shaffner responded to a push-button signal, ready for almost any kind of reasonable or unreasonable request for attention—including, she thought at first, this one.

Like most attractive hostesses, Ms. Shaffner was not unaccustomed to occasional maneuvers of machismo. By training and experience she knew how to cool the ardent without causing hard feelings. Sunglasses' approach was different from the usual pass. Less robust. More self-effacing. He said nothing, just handed her a folded slip of paper.

Ms. Shaffner assumed her pen pal was too shy to speak his declaration of affection out loud. Nevertheless, as she put it, "I thought he was trying to hustle me."

Since the customer is always right, or almost always, she tried to evade the issue by not reading the note on the spot. Her appreciative smile was designed to say she needed time to read and consider the proposal. However, the author's intentions were far less honorable than she had imagined.

"I stuffed the note in my pocket and he motioned I should take it out and read it." His gestures were insistent and demanding. Well, if that would make him happy . . .

Passenger R. Simmons, who happened to glance idly back toward the hostess while she read, recollected much later: "I saw her face drop. She looked bewildered and gulped." But he minded his own business.

Although the note was short, succinct, and legible, and Ms. Shaffner is not a slow reader, it took her time to get the message.

It demanded ten thousand twenty-dollar bills and two sport parachutes or else 305, passengers and crew would be blown up.

"Could this be for real?" she was asking herself, when D. B. answered by snapping open his briefcase. In it were two menacing red cylinders attached to coils of wire. It speaks well for Ms. Shaffner's grace under pressure that her only visible reaction was a gulp.

It was a panicky time for plane people. There'd been an epidemic of skyjackings, and not long before an FBI attempt to shoot out tires of a kidnapped aircraft had resulted in three deaths. In this scary atmosphere, nobody— beginning with Ms. Shaffner, and including the legion of others to be involved—ever dared to assume D. B. was bluffing. Nobody ever was to know whether the threatening cylinders were real or make-believe bombs. Nobody was prepared to risk forty-two lives (forty-three if you count Cooper), as well as several million dollars' worth of three-engined Boeing 727.

So when the terrified young woman made her way to the

cockpit and gave Captain William Scott the man's written instructions, Scott immediately radioed the Seattle control tower for his instructions. Control in turn communicated with police and FBI, and with Don Nyrop, president of Northwest Airlines, asking for their instructions.

Nyrop to Scott: "Do whatever he demands."

Control to Scott: "FBI and police have advised no action be taken. Repeat. No action be taken."

Exactly what action Scott or any other member of the crew could have taken, nobody knows. If anybody had a rash impulse to become a hero or heroine, the orders from authority stopped it.

So far as the passengers were concerned, all systems were go as the plane continued on its scheduled course to Seattle. They were blissfully unaware of all the consternation on the ground. Even when Captain Scott's voice informed them that there would be some delay in landing because of minor mechanical difficulties, they accepted the news without question. The only traveler who knew about the negotiations with the authorities was D. B., and he wasn't talking.

The plane continued to go round and round in the air as a flock of Northwest employees besieged Seattle banks, collecting the required ten thousand twenties. Others were going around in circles trying to locate the two sets of parachutes the hijacker had demanded. All this took time, and D. B. would not allow the plane to land until everything was ready.

As the slow circling minutes turned to hours, tension began to mount among the passengers. Uneasiness grew into worry and burgeoned into fear that there was something seriously wrong with the plane, and that disaster lay ahead.

The only exception to the general nervousness was Cooper. One of his fellow travelers' contributions to the subsequent police investigation was, "He seemed kind of relaxed."

Part of the reason for the postponed landing was that when Northwest was ready with the cash and parachutes provided by the Air Force, the hijacker rejected the latter. He repeated his original demand for "sport" free-fall parachutes, the kind skydivers use to aim themselves at a target on the ground. This communication he dictated to Mucklow for delivery to Captain Scott.

Scott relayed the message. Then while the sporting gear was being looked for he reported.

Scott to Control: "The guy is getting antsy."

Control to Scott: "Impress on him we're not trying to stall."

Scott: "He's getting impatient. We're going to have to come up with them [the sport chutes] pretty quick."

By the time Seattle was able to comply and the aircraft began its descent to a far corner of the airport, the twenty-five-minute flight from Portland had taken more than three hours.

It was only after they had landed that the passengers discovered they were hostages with much worse things to worry about than plane failure. For the hostages and the hijacker alike, the moments after the plane taxied to a stop were the most dangerous thus far. No one could be sure

The hijacked 727 jetliner at Seattle-Tacoma International Airport. The parachutes and $200,000 in cash were delivered to the plane in the car shown at left.

what kind of reception the collective mind of the law had worked out for Flight 305. Was some kind of trap being laid? Would some eager beaver call D. B.'s hand? Was there a platoon of trigger-happy snipers ready to let loose a barrage of rifle fire?

At this stage, the passengers were rooting for the bomb carrier. They hoped that nobody would try to interfere with his nefarious scheme, lest this become their last

Thanksgiving day. Fortunately everything went smoothly and rapidly. The only hitch came when a Federal Aviation Administration official appeared and attempted to show Cooper the error of his ways.

Cooper's response was antsy. "Let's get this show on the road," he growled. Not a very original statement, but enough to brush off the FAA.

A brief glance into a laundry sack bulging with twenty-one pounds of twenty-dollar bills, and a more detailed inspection of the parachutes satisfied him. With an urgent wave of his hand he dismissed the occupants of the plane except for flight attendant Mucklow and the crew of the cockpit.

Keeping their distance, the officers of the law stood helplessly by while the hostages scrambled off the plane and headed gratefully toward their Thanksgiving dinners. The door of the plane closed, the jets roared and the 727 climbed up in a curtain of exhaust that ended this act of the drama.

Until now, the police and Department of Justice operatives had followed D.B.'s instructions almost to the letter, no matter how reluctantly. But they had no intention of letting him get away with his loot. By previous arrangement, a posse of three Air Force jets took off in the 727's contrails.

The first report to Seattle from the air trackers was that the plane was headed due south. South lay Oregon, California, Mexico and Latin America. Word was flashed to colleagues south to look for the fugitive flying machine. Within minutes the jets radioed that the 727 had changed its mind. It was now veering westward.

In Seattle, the freed hostages were not yet enjoying their turkey and stuffing. They were being subjected to a grilling by law officers, desperate to get some line on Cooper. They answered the investigators' questions as best they could, but not well enough to clue the police in. They had much more information to give in answer to the profoundly inane questions that TV reporters invariably ask survivors of any ordeal: "How did you feel when . . . ? Were you scared when . . . ? How scared were you?" But for practical purposes, the sum total of all the witnesses' testimony was: They really saw no evil, heard no evil.

In Seattle, official skull sessions tried to psych D. B. out, in search of his next gambit. Obviously he had to get off the plane somewhere. What wasn't so obvious was, where? They could deal with that one because a 727 would need more than a mile-long strip to land on. And they could figure pretty closely, knowing how much gas the aircraft had left, which airports were landing possibilities.

The parachutes stimulated a lot of head-scratching. Were they meant to mislead the law into thinking the hijacker was going to abandon the liner in flight, or were they a for-real part of his game plan? Was he out of his mind? Hop out at night? In a business suit? Into the snowstorm that swirled over the thickly forested mountain wilderness to the south and west? Was he the kind of nut who wanted to leave his footprint in the sands of crime by going out in a blaze of suicidal glory? Or had he come to his senses and realized that he couldn't get away with his loot and chosen to end it all? Anyway, why two parachutes? Crazy, man, crazy, no matter what else.

Pilot William Scott and flight attendants Florence Shaffner (center) and Tina Mucklow (right) described their experiences to newsmen the following day.

Meanwhile, back in the plane, D. B. was dictating answers to some of their questions. Tina Mucklow wrote them down and transported them to Captain Scott. D. B. ordered Scott to head for Mexico. Tina shuttled back from cockpit to tail with news that the plane lacked the fuel to make Mexico. D. B. accepted this news without protest. Another dictation to Mucklow for Scott revised the flight plan. Scott was to head south toward Portland and then west to Reno for refueling, maintain altitude below ten thousand feet, keep flaps down, cruise at 200 m.p.h.

This time D. B. escorted Mucklow down the length of empty plane and locked her with the new course into the cockpit, ordering all concerned to stay put. This was to be the last anyone saw of him.

There was, however, another sign of his existence somewhat later. A red light flashed on the control panel. It signaled that the ship's rear boarding ramp was being unlatched. The time, Scott noted, was 7:50. At 8:10 a second light signaled a fully extended ramp. This was not the way the 727 was designed to fly and Scott was having his difficulties. For want of anything better to say he called back on the public address system to his sole passenger: "Anything we can do for you?"

There was no answer.

The aircraft was approaching the wild wooded slopes of the Cascade Mountains. This area in southern Washington, where Lake Merwin is formed by the Lewis River, is rugged backpack country. The closest sign of civilization is tiny Woodland, Washington, which is only a few air minutes north of metropolitan Portland, where D. B. Cooper

24

had bought his one-way ticket that afternoon. If D. B. had indeed jumped at 8:10, around Woodland—as the law was to assume—he had not only injured Northwest Airlines out of two hundred thousand dollars, but added the insult of getting almost a whole round trip for a one-way fare. At any rate the crew didn't come out of the cockpit until the plane landed at Reno, some hours later. The only evidence D. B. had left of his pioneering effort was one set of parachutes. Sunglasses, brown suit, sack of twenties, briefcase, twin red cylinders and man had vanished into the thin, black, snowy, seven-below-zero air blowing at two hundred miles an hour.

The population of Woodland soared astronomically as the town became the headquarters for what was proclaimed in the nation's press and on TV screens as a four-state manhunt. From Woodland, organized official hunters—including a Third Army Cavalry and a United States Army detachment from Fort Lewis—and unorganized, unofficial hunters slogged through 250 square miles of snow-covered, primeval-forested Cowlitz County. A pair of army helicopters chopped through the air over the treetops in which a parachute would almost certainly have been snared.

In return for their strenuous efforts to enforce the law, the members of the posse got nothing but unappreciative protests from fur trappers who complained that hordes of searchers were bad for their business. After a week, the search was called off, on account of the weather. As Cowlitz County Undersheriff McDowell had theorized, "We're either looking for a parachute or a hole in the ground." Clearly either one or the other would become more readily

25

A deputy sheriff and an FBI agent continue the search for Cooper by helicopter in the vicinity of Woodland, Washington.

visible when the winter was over. But many suns later, when the concealing snow was gone, neither parachute nor hole in the ground, nor any remnant of D. B.'s luggage, the treasure, or D. B. himself made an appearance.

On the second anniversary of D. B.'s death-defying dive,

Julius Mattson, head of the Portland office of the FBI, commemorated his agency's frustration with what can be interpreted as a tribute to the frustrator: "We know nothing more about him today than we did on November 24, 1971."

So that while the file on Cooper is and will stay technically open, in the hope that some flaw will turn up in what has remained a perfect crime, it is, practically speaking, closed. This leaves the solution of the mystery to the deductions of amateurs. Our guess as to the possibilities and probabilities is at least as good as those of the failed professional thief-catchers.

One supposition that can be eliminated from the start is that the police overlooked any clues to identifying D. B. Anyone who had had any glimpse of him looked vainly at mug shots. Fingerprints? There weren't any. Not even on the note he had written? Well, maybe there were latents on the note, and certainly a sample of his handwriting, but these aren't in D. B.'s file. This isn't because the police had overlooked them, but because they were not available for microscopic analysis. The hijacker was careful to take his note back after it had been read.

Logic dictates that given the frightful conditions under which the leap was made no parachutist had any chance to survive. In his brown suit, D. B. would have frozen to death before he landed. The fact, say some, that his body wasn't found doesn't prove he isn't mouldering away, or that someone hasn't found him, filled in the hole he made when he hit, and walked away with the money. Probable. Possible.

But suppose, just suppose there was a method to his mad bail-out, the same attention to detail revealed in every other stage of his modus operandi. Suppose D. B. was an experienced skydiver, one of those daredevils who gets his kicks out of free-falling to a target. Suppose he delayed getting his hands on the two hundred thousand because he had to have the kind of jumping gear he was familiar with. And suppose further that this careful planner had prepared for his coup by practice jumping to a preset mark over the uninhabited terrain where he disappeared. Under the suit, couldn't he have been wired against the cold? And who can say whether there wasn't a confederate waiting to ski, snowshoe or jeep him away to safety?

Improbable? Impossible? Well, maybe. But then, isn't the Cooper caper all of those things? Isn't that why it is the only one of its kind? If it weren't, the solution wouldn't still be up for grabs.

MURDER ON FIFTH AVENUE:
The Strangling of Serge Rubinstein

•

EVEN THE MOST AVERAGE, run-of-the-mill playboy will make headlines when he's been murdered in his mansion, especially if he is sexily dressed for the occasion in black silk pajamas and is discovered by a genuine English butler. When the victim who fitted these particulars happened to be someone as world infamous as Serge Rubinstein, the newspapers couldn't have asked for a more sensational story.

The New York City police, who had to find the hands that took the mansion master's breath away permanently, were not so enthusiastic. But if the strangler has never been turned up, it is not because the investigators didn't do everything humanly possible. Their problem was that before they could answer, "Who did it?" they had to figure out, "Which Serge Rubinstein was killed?"

This was infinitely more difficult than it sounds. Although there was never any doubt that the stubby (5'7") body on the bedroom floor was the mortal remnant of *the* Serge Rubinstein—the same Serge whose rich, full, fraudulent forty-six years had been voluminously pictured and printed in the papers—still, in those forty-six years he had played many different parts.

When butler William Worthy's phone call brought the Sixty-seventh Precinct cops to the marbled halls of 814 Fifth Avenue on the morning of January 27, 1955, they didn't need a next-of-kin identification. The adhesive tape that sealed his lips, the Venetian blind cords in which he was trussed up, altered him somewhat, but it was Serge Rubinstein all right. And there on the wall was redundant confirmation—a blown-up photograph of Serge dressed for a costume ball, in the cocked hat and imperial uniform of Napoleon.

The tape and cords turned out to be useless as clues. And too many people had visited the third-floor bedroom for fingerprints to be of any value. At this initial stage of the investigation the detectives paid little attention to the Napoleon blowup and ignored the statue of the emperor prominent in the room. So he would have liked to be Napoleon. So what? So it told more about Serge, and what made him go, and what led him to his death, than all the subsequent investigation was to reveal.

Of course the Napoleon clue, if it can be called that, was only symbolic. Bonaparte had a much more one-track mind. The power and glory he sought were only in war. Serge was a man of many-sided interests. He was, among

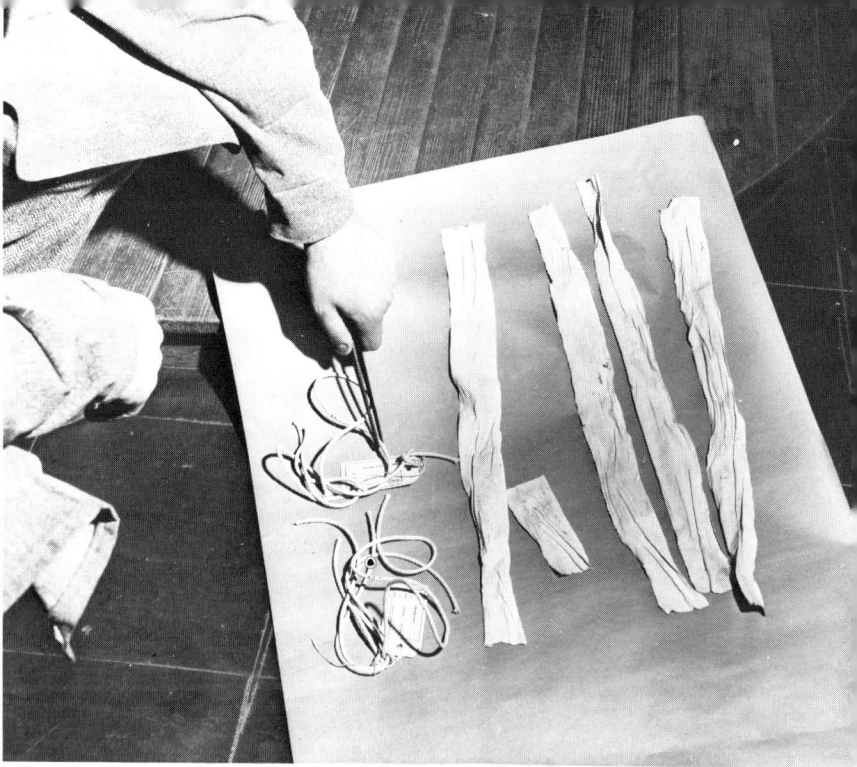

Police examination of the physical evidence in the Rubinstein case—these pieces of cord and tape—provided no clue to the murderer's identity.

other things, a whiz-kid banker; a grownup international financier; an ex-convict; a passionate collector of art, cover girls, senators, representatives, ambassadors, politicians, and socialites of high and low degree.

Serge's versatility was known to the public and the police, mostly because he assiduously advertised himself. None of his activities, however nefarious, ever resulted in a

Serge Rubinstein.

"no comment" to reporters. Unlike other glory seekers, Serge accentuated the negative—the amoral, dubious and rascally aspects of his exploits. The tarnished self-image he helped create made him a continuing headlined story in the papers. Of course he didn't tell it all. How much of what he told was true, or how much of it he believed himself, still remains to be seen.

According to his own account—the year he was killed he was trying to have his autobiography published—he had been forced, like his hero Napoleon, to retreat from Russia. Of course there were differences. Serge was ten years old, and he fled not the czar's army, but the Bolsheviks. Unlike Napoleon he was an innocent target of Russian wrath. The Reds were after him because they disapproved of his father's job as consultant to the mad monk Rasputin, adviser to the czarina.

Clad in a size eight fur coat—he was small for his age—Serge took off over the iced Gulf of Finland in a three-horse troika, the Reds steaming on his trail. Sewn into the lining was a czar's ransom in rubies, diamonds, emeralds and sapphires. And his underwear was embroidered with rubles and securities. Several months later, the jeweled boy was joined by his parents and his big brother Andre in Stockholm.

When Serge was about to turn fifteen, the Rubinsteins were living in Vienna, birthplace of psychoanalysis. Here he asked for a birthday present which would have confounded the parent of any adolescent, even one accustomed to dealing with Rasputin.

The gift? Analysis by one of the founding fathers of that art, Dr. Alfred Adler.

Why not a Rolls Royce or a increased allowance or roller skates?

"Because," Serge tells us, "I was afraid I was developing an inferiority complex."

Evidently his dad was convinced. But after only a couple or three sessions, Serge got off the couch for good. He remembered the experience vividly enough to quote Adler's parting words verbatim. "If I cure you," the great healer said, "you'll be just ordinary. The way you are now, you'll be driven by ambition and desires."

Could even the renowned Dr. Adler have restored Serge to healthy ordinariness? If one were to judge by the rest of Serge's extraordinary career, it would have been a miracle. But if his ambition and desires had been directed toward less self-serving and more altruistic goals, he might have died of old age.

Thus far, nothing in his dossier was of any help to the police. Serge had not yet—as a teenager—succeeded in making any enemies except for the Bolsheviks. And they had dropped out of his life after losing the horse race on ice.

By the time he was eighteen Serge had made a modest beginning toward being cordially disliked. He was an honor student at Cambridge University in England. His big brother Andre had advanced the money for his education. The relationship between the brothers was strained when Serge neglected to repay the loan. It broke not long after Serge came of age, when Andre sued to reclaim a couple of million dollars he charged Serge had stolen from him.

Not until he was twenty-three did Serge make a major first stride toward collecting enemies—at least, the first giant step on record. Many hard feelings were aroused when he gave himself a birthday present—$1 million. He was able to be so generous because despite his tender years he had become the hard-nosed manager of a Paris bank, Franco-Asiatique. Banking prodigy Rubinstein was thus in

the right place (where the money was) at the right time—
when a little inside information plus a lot of unscrupu-
lousness could be converted into cash.

Some years earlier, the Chiang Kai-shek government of
China had defaulted on a bond issue which had been offered to the public through Franco-Asiatique. The problem
faced by banker Rubinstein was that China needed money
again and wanted Franco-Asiatique to sell a second series
of bonds. Well, obviously, investors would be less than
eager to buy the new bonds when the old were worthless.

There was nothing particularly original about Serge's solution: Let China guarantee the value of the second issue
by depositing the interest in the bank, and he would rec-
ommend to the Franco-Asiatique management that the
deal be made. This was done.

The rest is banking history. Serge surreptitiously bought
up the defaulted bonds for just a little more than their
worth—nothing—and when China delivered the million-
dollar interest on the new bonds to Franco-Asiatique's
manager, M. Rubinstein, he turned it over to the new
owner of the old bonds, M. Rubinstein.

As he proudly summed up the transaction: "I had the
bonds and I had the money. I just paid myself off."

Illegal? No. Unethical? Yes, by the rules of the banking
community regarding employee conduct. But then, the investors who'd held the worthless paper could not have held
Franco-Asiatique or Serge or China in high ethical esteem.

The result of the slippery scheme was that Serge became
celebrated as a financial whiz. And the French government
began a three-year effort to kick him out of the country.

But Serge insisted that his ultimate expulsion from France was not really because of his double-dealing, but because he was irresistible to a certain titled lady: "Pierre Laval [French Premier] was jealous of my *friendship* [italics by Serge] with his mistress, a French Marquise."

Having begun to accumulate French ill-wishers through his wizardry in romance and finance, Serge promptly began to add to their number a legion of Englishmen. These new enemies included the management and the stockholders of Chosen Mining, Ltd., a London company that owned gold mines in Korea. It was a highly regarded concern in the City, England's financial center—a splendid investment for a young man who'd just made a million. But Serge had no intention of investing his bundle. Little Serge decided to rule giant Chosen by ruining it—an incredibly risky enterprise for any market mastermind except Serge.

He developed a method for eliminating risks that became known as "the Rubinstein Squeeze." That's how *Fortune*, the magazine of big business, described it in an obituary four months after his death. Simultaneously deploring and eulogizing his shady shrewdness, the article commemorated the unique position Serge had achieved in the big business community. *Fortune*'s readers learned the Rubinstein strategy for avoiding taking chances: "I never speculated unless the elements of speculation were removed and I control or have the man who turns the wheels on my payroll."

Judging by his long and successful career, the strategy was foolproof. Viewing it in hindsight, Serge had risked only one thing—his neck.

Of course the tactics of controlling the wheels or the wheel-turners differed from operation to operation. In the case of the Chosen Corporation outsider Rubinstein found someone on the inside who sold him information on how the Chosen's wheels were turning in an illegal direction. This valuable material he gave away free to the press. Bankers, brokers, and Chosen Co. stockholders were appalled by the allegations of hanky-panky, which were denied by management, then confirmed by investigation. In the ensuing scandal, one board member went to jail for having had his hand in the company till. Others barely managed to stay out of prison.

Serge did not go unrewarded for exposing corruption. As Chosen's executives toppled, so did the stocks. When the latter were at their all-time low, Serge bought control of the immensely profitable company.

It is impossible to know just how many millions this maneuver made for Serge, or how many more people he had convinced the world would be a better place without him. If he had been killed then, in 1933, matters would have been somewhat simpler for the police than they were when he was strangled. Back then they would have had to look no further than the victims of his Old World schemes— thousands, to be sure, but nothing to compare to the hordes of suspects he would amass when he emigrated to America in 1938.

The U.S.A. was not exactly a Welcome Wagon for a would-be immigrant whom the French had found undesirable and finally managed to get rid of. (There was some truth in Serge's claim that he had voluntarily left France—

The Fifth Avenue mansion where
Rubinstein was found dead.

the truth being that he hadn't been bodily hurled out.) But
American Immigration couldn't summarily shut out the af-
fable, obviously affluent young newcomer who, despite all
previous evidence of his Russian birth, swore he was a Portuguese citizen. The Portuguese passport he presented to
the United States immigration officers in 1938 was made
out to and signed by the bearer, Serge Manuel Rubinstein
de Ronello.

This bewildering transformation needed some fancy explanation, especially under oath. Serge Manuel swore it
wasn't a transformation. He'd always been Portuguese but
he hadn't revealed it because he was guarding the family
honor. Now he had no choice but to expose the skeleton in
the Rubinstein–de Ronello closet. The awful truth was that
his dear, saintly mother had sinned once, and . . . well
. . . he was illegitimate . . . a love child . . . the product
of a liaison between her and a Senhor de Ronello, a native
Portuguese.

This soap opera stuff apparently so fascinated the Immigration fellows that they let Serge in. But the spell didn't
last. In later episodes we find them trying to deport him.
Serge fought them off for more than a decade with the best
legal talent money could buy, and a lot of surreptitious
help from his friends.

It is possible that among the legion of Serge's intimate
friends—some of them highly visible public figures, others

who preferred anonymity—there were those who helped keep him in the country because they honestly felt he was a desirable alien. But from what we know of Serge, it is more likely favors were bought—with money or with information about where bodies were buried. In this kind of deal, what happens when the buyer feels he isn't getting his money's worth?

By January, 1955, Serge's time in America was running out. He was due to appear in court a month later for a deportation hearing. The word was out that nothing could help keep him here this time. He'd given proof of his undesirability with one conviction and a prison term for draft evasion and a narrow escape from a second for mail fraud, and Immigration had found proof that his Portuguese passport was a forgery. In all fairness, no amount of influence could help beat these raps.

Not notorious for his sense of fairness, Serge may well have put the squeeze on his friends. Always amply supplied with inside information, he may have threatened to put it to use. Would blackmail have been beyond Serge? Might it not have provoked the retaliatory, fatal squeeze on his neck? No concrete evidence. Merely a speculation which opens another can of possible suspects.

Rubinstein's efforts to remain in the United States had other ramifications. Brother Andre, busy in the courts for years trying to nail his sibling as a crook, sued for defamation of their mother's character. But Serge's preposterous claim to love-childhood seemed not to affect his tender relationship with his mother. In fact, she occupied the top floor bedroom of the quintuplex the night he was mur-

Police carry Rubinstein's body down the staircase of his lavish home.

dered. Another permanent member of the mansion was her sister.

Both elderly ladies did their best to assist the police investigation. Mrs. Rubinstein remembered hearing the sound of disputing voices from her son's quarters about 2:00 A.M. (The medical examiner established the time of death as between 2:00 and 5:00 A.M.) She had called down, but there was no answer. Her eighty-two-year-old sister reported that she had waked during the night and had seen "a mysterious woman" prowling through the hall. Investigation revealed that the mystery woman was really butler Worthy in a bathrobe, making his closing rounds. And the disputing voices Mrs. Rubinstein heard only confirmed that it was not unusual for Serge to have secret meetings in the wee hours with anonymous visitors of both sexes.

Homicide concluded early in the investigation that the butler didn't do it, nor the members of the household staff. They also eliminated robbery as a motive: valuables were not taken, nor was there any sign of a forcible entry. Having eliminated these possibilities, they deduced that the killer was someone on close enough terms with Serge to gain admission to the mansion. But who?

Unearthing Serge's personal and private list of names and addresses should have helped the detectives. Ordinarily a victim's little black book gives investigators a lead to his intimate life—to possible suspects. The trouble with Serge's list was that it filled not one pocket-sized book but three enormous loose-leaf ledgers. The police never made the contents of these volumes public. It's doubtful whether doing so would have helped the investigation in any way, and it certainly would have embarrassed a lot of people with a lot of clout.

None of the prominent personages with whom Serge had mingled rushed forward to help the authorities revenge their "friend." He was gone and forgotten. Among those absent at his funeral were the guests who had glittered at his lavish wedding reception in Washington—as well as the bride, who had divorced him for physical cruelty almost before all the presents were opened. Among those who had been at the wedding, the gossip columnists reported, were nine ambassadors, dozens of senators and representatives, scores of lobbyists, political bosses, scads of screen and stage stars, scions of society (high and cafe) and Wall Street luminaries too numerous to count.

As for the shadowy types he had on his secret payroll, you couldn't realistically expect them to mourn his passing in public. The police would have welcomed an opportunity to chat with any of his stable of inside informers: for instance, the guy who had tipped him off that New York City was going to take over the BMT subway. Or the one who'd slipped him the advance dope about the merger between Western Union and Postal Telegraph. Serge had bragged about the killings he had made on these deals. But he never revealed his sources.

Had they been located they would have soared to the top of the suspect list. In the annals of bribery it is not unprecedented for the bribed to demand greater remuneration, be refused and get violent. Could be that on the agenda of Serge's last meeting was a motion to divide the profits more equally and Serge voted it down.

Serge's little black bookkeeping did not identify his stable of informers, so despite arduous police efforts, this potentially rich field for investigation did not pan out. The detectives cannot be criticized for failing to strike pay dirt. *Fortune* magazine's expert researchers, who dug for the facts about Rubinstein's deals, could come up with only what he had put on record. And they disclaimed any responsibility for the accuracy of his statements.

When a victim is an ex-convict, an obvious place to look for clues is among jailbirds. The reasoning is simple. A man with a criminal past is likely to have a criminal present. It is reasonable to assume that among the underworld characters with whom Serge exercised in the prison yard at Lewisburg Penitentiary in 1947 were some capable of murder. This may have been why the only business associate of Rubinstein to speak to the press, stockbroker Stanley K. Stanley, told reporters: "I believe it was a mob job." But Mr. Stanley also reaffirmed that to his knowledge Serge had many business enemies.

Serge had been convicted for a new dodge, avoiding the World War II draft. There were plenty of other draft dodgers, but none of them in his evasive class. Before the jury found him guilty he had managed to have his 1-A classification—"immediately available for service"—changed fifteen times. While one set of wires was being pulled to keep him in the country, another set was tugging him out of the army.

According to Mr. Stanley, Rubinstein was reluctant to serve because "He was a neutral." But he couldn't have been all that neutral. One of his claims to deferment was that, as the owner of the Taylorcraft Corporation, which made airplanes, he was indispensable to the American war effort on the home production front.

The court, however, judged his purchase of Taylorcraft a phony scheme to stay out of uniform. Not only was Serge convicted, but the president of Taylorcraft, whom he involved, was found guilty of complicity in the fraud and also went to jail. Though he was probably a willing conspirator he could certainly not have had much affection for Serge. But like the other trails the police had followed, the investigation of Serge's prison contacts led nowhere.

In the last year of his life Serge was involved in several happenings which he wouldn't talk to the press about. These were also probed by police in the search for suspects—without results. He was beaten up by two men whom he could not or would not identify. And unidentified sources told reporters that they saw Serge chase a man into a telephone booth and throw thousand-dollar bills at him. The police had less trouble authenticating the gossip item that Rubinstein had escorted seven beautiful women to the New Year's Eve White Russian Ball, just weeks before he was murdered.

This last event, a flamboyant example of Serge's prowess as a ladies' man, put the murder in the sensational category of a crime of passion. None of the other facts of his life which were laid bare were as absorbing to the public.

Since the police were only human, they gave this aspect of his career particular attention. They discovered that Serge rarely confined his attentions to fewer than a half-dozen women at one time. He had a habit of providing his

Serge Rubinstein and friend, singer Betty Reed, at Nino's La Rue.

current favorites with keys to his front door, and when he changed them for a new batch, he changed the lock.

The discards were of obvious interest because everybody hates being rejected. But of more immediate interest were the then current crop of key holders. They could let themselves in. Likewise, anyone who could borrow, beg or steal one of these keys could get into the house.

In the "hell-hath-no-fury-like-a-woman-scorned" phase of the investigation, the police established that the last person to be seen with the victim was model Estelle Gardner. She had supped and danced with Serge at a very exclusive and exceptionally expensive night spot, Nino's La Rue. A cab driver who picked them up there remembered the time, 12:30 A.M., and he had no trouble remembering his fares because Serge had borrowed a quarter from him to tip Nino's doorman. He said he'd driven his fares to 814 Fifth, and saw them enter the house.

Miss Gardner took the story up from there. Yes, she'd been with Serge for a nightcap until 1:30, and then had gone home. And she proved it. The police questioned Pat Wray, another of Serge's companions, and heard from her that at 2:30 A.M. Serge had phoned and invited her to drop over. She had respectfully declined the invitation. And that was the last time anyone heard from him. Sometime during the next two to three hours he was killed.

The fifty detectives assigned to the case had the pleasure of meeting some five hundred beautiful women before they finished checking out the harem listings in Serge's address books. But that's all they got from the discarded woman–jealous boyfriend theory.

Then came an anonymous tip that set Homicide off on the trail of the crime-for-profit suspects. BREAKTHROUGH IN RUBE STRANGLING, the tabloids screamed. POLICE HOLD EX CON. ADMITS SERGE SNATCH SCHEME.

It looked bad for felon Herman Scholz. Though he was the only suspect whose name was not included in Serge's address book, he became Rubinstein Enemy Number 1 in the press and in the district attorney's office. The fifty-year-old, jockey-sized, part-time hire-a-car chauffeur had a long petty criminal record. When the police broke into his home they discovered an arsenal—submachine guns, pistols, revolvers, blackjacks and switchblades. Scholz told a pretty unlikely story. He professed to have collected the lethal gadgets because he was planning to rob a bank.

The skeptical cops couldn't connect the shooting irons to the Rubinstein killing, but they had another link, at once more innocent and more sinister. Stashed away in Scholz's room, along with the armaments, was a bundle of clippings reporting in detail the mystery of the murder in the mansion.

Of course, there's no law says a person can't cut up a newspaper. But the police hammered away at this hobby of Scholz's. Scholz finally confessed that another of his ambitions was to kidnap Serge and hold him for ransom. Moreover, he admitted that he had taken steps to put the plan into practice. For three months he had been watching the Rubinstein mansion.

Scholz was held as a material witness in twenty-five thousand dollars' bail. A spokesman for the district attorney's office proclaimed: "Scholz conveyed his kidnapping plan to persons, members of the underworld, who in our very definite opinion committed the murder."

Scholz did not deny he had conveyed his plan to col-

Suspect Herman Scholz escorted from the police station by detectives, for further questioning at the DA's office.

leagues, but he swore they had rejected him and his dream of the big time. He was only saving the clippings to show the scoffers what a golden opportunity they had missed. They'd been beaten to the punch by the murder.

The authorities thought that the accused hadn't told all. Judge Jonah J. Goldstein peered down from his bench at the diminutive dreamer and said: "You're too small to have tried kidnapping by yourself." (Previous to this legal opinion there had been no minimum height requirement for kidnappers.)

As time passed, Assistant DA Alexander Herman began to hedge the prosecutor's first firm conviction: "As to what we have now, it looks like an underworld job, a snatch which went wrong."

And that's where the matter rested in 1955 and where it still rests. The snatch theory got no further than the woman-scorned theory.

Murder mystery fans generally enjoy an after-the-fact advantage over real or fictional detectives. They can usually prove they're smarter than the professionals by picking out the flaws in police procedures which prevented the solution of the crime.

In the Rubinstein case the amateur detective is as stumped as the one who gets paid. The New York police asked the right questions, beginning with "Who had a motive for killing Serge? Did he have any enemies?" And that's about as far as they or anyone else could get.

Serge had campaigned all his life to achieve his pre-eminent position as a candidate for murder. There were just too many people whom he had provided with persuasive reasons to vote for his death. There were just too many suspects.

The Rubinstein murderer remained free not because he'd carefully covered up his crime, but because he had an accomplice—the victim. By a lifetime of accumulating potential murderers, Serge made it impossible to solve his murder. If justice was never done—well, there's a kind of justice in that.

THE TEN HOT OLD MASTERS:
The Brooklyn Museum Art Theft

•

ALMOST EVERY OCCUPATION, vocation and profession has its time-tested how-to-succeed rules. And there are all kinds of schools and colleges where ambitious young people can learn the prescribed way to shinny up the ropes to the top. Relatively new among such institutions of learning are the academies in which career-minded policemen study how to circumvent robbers.

So far as can be ascertained, there are no accredited institutions of learning for robbers—unless you include prisons, where the course of study is less than formal. But even without textbooks, would-be masters of the criminal arts learn to practice the basic rules of how-not-to-be-caught-by-the-police.

Although police and criminals have opposing goals, the

activities of both sides are guided by identical rules—like any contest. Police game plans are based on the regulation dos and don'ts of their opponents, and vice versa.

Among the fundamentals learned by both teams is that the safest way to succeed at stealing is: Steal money, provided it's not in large denominations. All cash is green, not identifiable; possession and/or use of dollars—unlike, say, heroin—is not a crime. All other loot is less cool. Hot stuff requires the services of a fence, a middleman who discounts the value of the goods, whether they're precious gems or bonds or TV sets. He in turn seeks a customer for whom the price has to be right. This class of consumer is bound to be more picky about a purchase than even Ralph Nader. During such transactions, no matter how gingerly the merchandise is handled, all concerned can get burned.

Nevertheless there are some criminals who violate accepted rules with impunity. Mostly they don't get caught, though they specialize in acquiring the hottest, most easily identifiable, least salable loot there is—rare, one-of-a-kind works of art.

On the positive side of stealing paintings, there's something to be said. Once out of the frame a painting is easily transported. Canvas doesn't weigh much; it can be rolled, folded, tucked out of sight under almost any clothing other than a bikini. It's true that a masterpiece in square inches is generally worth less than the work of the same artist measured in feet, but it's worth stealing. For example, the largest of the ten paintings stolen from the Brooklyn Museum in 1933 was twenty-four by eighteen inches. But one of them, *The Ascension of Christ* by Peter Paul Rubens,

The Ascension of Christ, by Peter Paul Rubens.

might bring some three million dollars on the open market—if it were available.

The Brooklyn Museum robbery is a kind of classic example of evildoing in the art world. One of its unique qualities is how simple it was. Another is the extent to which the police were baffled. They weren't even able to find someone they could suspect unjustly. Still another is that after they had succeeded at first, the crooks for some reason tried again, and again—twice more, fruitlessly. Of course, it might not have been the same mob. The police were never sure. There was some reason to think yes, and some to think no.

The first clue that there was something amiss at the Brooklyn Museum was a rope dangling from a fourth-story window to the ground. Precisely how long it had been there, in the glare of the headlights of cars rolling along Washington Avenue, nobody knows. Perhaps if some passerby or motorist had seen it, he would have thought it had something to do with the remodeling work being done on the museum.

It was finally noticed at 3:00 A.M. Sunday, April 30, 1933, by alert night watchman Frank Walsh, one of the eight after-hours guardians of the museum's treasures. Mr. Walsh discovered that the rope was anchored to a newel post on the fourth-floor landing. With his colleagues he searched the fourth-floor gallery. Nothing was missing. In strict observance of the institution's regulations he reported the happening in writing.

The Walsh report was put where it belonged, on the desk of his boss, museum executive Joseph Seabeck. Mr. Seabeck had Sunday off, and thus didn't get to read it until some time on Monday. His superior, Director William Fox, was at his post when the museum opened at 2:00 P.M.

Sunday, but nobody thought to tell him about the mysterious rope.

It wasn't until 3:00 P.M. on Sunday that fifth-floor gallery attendant Charles Hansen noticed that ten of the frames hanging on the walls of his appointed round were empty. Why it took him so long is hard to explain. In justice to him, it should be pointed out that his job was to look out for people inclined to steal paintings, not to look at paintings.

At any rate, before Fox learned of the theft, and somebody remembered the rope, and a connection was made, much time had passed. Too much time, in the angry opinion of Deputy Chief Inspector Vincent J. Sweeney. He complained that the police department wasn't informed until the next day. The press reported:

DELAY OVER ROPE CLUE

CHECKS ART RECOVERY

In the chief's own words, "The trail is cold."

Of course the trail was chillier than it would have been if they'd been told sooner. But there is reason to suspect that Sweeney might have been copping a premature plea. He laid heavy stress upon the difficulties his boys faced: "There has been only a meager description of the suspects." In fact there was less than a meager description. There was none at all. Nobody had seen or heard anything suspicious. There were fingerprints on the vacated frames, but they were so jumbled as to be useless.

This did not prevent the police from coming up with some highly theoretical suspects, good for a headline:

INTERNATIONAL CROOKS GET MUSEUM TREASURE

Any particular crooks? The police couldn't be more specific than this: "A band of art thieves in touch with markets [unspecified] and collectors [unmentioned] all over the world."

They had reason to believe—they didn't give it—that this was the same gang that had stolen five rare miniatures from New York's Metropolitan Museum of Art in 1927. In that case, the modus operandi had been different. The crooks had also walked off with the frames. That was only because the Met's frames were studded with real diamonds, the police noted to explain the discrepancy.

Sweeney also credited this company of superthieves with having scored against galleries, museums and private collections in European capitals. But despite all the hypothetical accomplishments of this hypothetical gang, the police were far from helpless, Sweeney assured the press: "The department is equipped to carry on the hunt for the treasures through the education of Detective Lieutenant Thomas Dugan who has been studying to become an art connoisseur since the theft of the Metropolitan paintings."

Without withdrawing his endorsement of Lieutenant Dugan, whom he had borrowed from a Manhattan precinct, Sweeney cautioned against optimism: "Art thefts generally take many years for solution. Art thieves are the cleverest in the world."

There is much in what the chief said. The folks who specialize in art thievery have achieved a distinction matched by no other evildoers. They have their own magazine—a publication exclusively devoted to stolen works of art.

It is the brainchild of an enterprising French businessman who saw a legal way to make money on art thefts. Called *The Official International of Stolen Paintings and Objects of Art*, it is to art fanciers what *Sports Illustrated* is to sports fans. Museums, galleries, private collectors all over the world subscribe—fifty dollars annually—for its descriptions and photographs of stolen art treasures.

Police were nagged by reporters to explain inexplicable circumstances, and they properly passed the buck to the museum officials. The press cornered a curator with: "Why did it take the fifth-floor guard so long to discover the paintings were missing?" And he answered with a condensed course in art history: "Pictures have often been hung upside down in galleries and neither public nor attendants have noticed." This doesn't seem to say much for pictures, the public, the attendants or for that matter, the curators who hang exhibits.

Though the police theories of who did the deed were vague, they were on much firmer ground with the hypothesis of how it was done.

Deduction: The thieves had entered the premises on Saturday along with less acquisitive art lovers and had stayed on after closing in any number of possible hiding places.

Deduction: There were at least three malefactors in the museum. Evidence? The sixty-foot rope was found to be made up of three twenty-foot segments. It followed that each crook had entered the building with one segment wound around under his clothing.

Mystery: Why did they take these particular pictures? Conjecture: They had an order from a particular buyer. Or perhaps they were such consummate connoisseurs that they selected works they knew were in demand by many no-questions-asked buyers.

It was Sweeney's opinion that since the works were foreign-made, patriotic foreign dealers might be eager to buy them in order to return them to where they came from. National pride has been an established motive for art theft since the heisting of the Mona Lisa from the Louvre in 1911. The Louvre is of course French. But the smiling lady of the portrait is Italian. And the fifteenth-century master Leonardo da Vinci, who painted the most famous grimace of all time on her face, was Italian. The unregenerate thief was Italian too. When caught, he proudly proclaimed: "I would be unworthy of Italy if I did not try to return to her this masterpiece. I did it to revenge Napoleon's depredations on Italian art."

The New York police also had precedents for assigning the blame to foreigners. When a bunch of paintings were taken from Buckingham Palace in 1930, the English press charged it was the work of American crooks conspiring with conscienceless American art dealers.

The Brooklyn Museum haul came at an inauspicious time for the police. It was the climax of a series of raids on New York's high-toned art neighborhood alley—the East Fifty-seventh Street art galleries. None of the treasures had been recovered. There were no arrests. The gallery owners were furious.

So the police tried very hard. Interrogating all 125 employees of the museum got them nowhere. Descriptions of the missing ten were cabled to European authorities. Ports of exit were watched. Intense attention was paid to the only evidence—beside the empty frames—that crime had been committed, the egress rope.

Who'd be most likely to employ this hazardous method of escape? Logically, persons with a special kind of athletic ability and training. This suggested acrobats or aerialists. Where are they most likely to be found? Under the Big Top. These propositions were supported by the discovery that the rope was the kind used in circuses. Find the circus to which it belonged, the police reasoned, and they'd be on the way to a solution of the burglary.

Unfortunately, the rope lead didn't prove out. As Captain James Pritchard, Sweeney's second in command, explained: "It is also the sort of rope used in shifting stage scenery, in dumbwaiters, in dry cleaning establishments, and in flag halyards, though such halyards are not usually that thick."

Ringling Bros. & Barnum & Bailey went uninvestigated while thirty detectives probed antique stores, obscure galleries and junk shops. Ten more, under the supervision of Lieutenant Dugan, enlisted the services of the Secret Service and customs inspectors to scrutinize vessels departing from New York harbor.

Two weeks after the theft Director Fox advertised a reward of two thousand dollars for the arrest and conviction of the crooks. Recovery of the plunder was not mentioned. There was no response to the offer.

Meanwhile, the museum took steps to make sure it couldn't happen again. All employees were ordered to shape up. With all possible security precautions taken, the museum was to be invulnerable—well, almost invulnerable, as time would prove.

Three months after the first robbery a second attempt was made. The fourth-floor gallery watchman spotted a shadowy intruder, sounded the alarm and gave chase. The would-be robber beat him down the stairs and escaped through an open window. All that the police could learn from the winded watchman was that the suspect was about twenty-five years old and toted a pistol.

Obviously the police had reason to wonder if there was a connection between incursions one and two. Was the second intruder a member of the same band? Or was he an amateur inspired by the success of the professionals? Whatever the answers were, it was embarrassing.

Just forty-eight hours later, the underworld was again guilty of contempt for the police. Once again, in the dead of night, there was somebody in the fourth-floor gallery for no good reason. His stealthy footsteps were overheard by an alert guard who tiptoed to a telephone to call the police. In answer, a hundred on- and off-duty police surrounded the building. But the quarry was as vigilant as the hunters. He got away without being seen. Once again, out of an open window. Once again, down a dangling rope—the same length and make of rope the thieves slid down in caper number one.

What could the men in blue do but suffer in silence and worry about the possibility of number four? And there was indeed going to be another robbery at the museum, but it wasn't to happen till long after Sweeney, Dugan, et al. had retired—not until 1974.

Fra Angelico   'Annunciation'

Rubens   'Christ's Ascension'

13 x 11 in.   Panel   33 x 28 c/m   7 x 15½ in.   Panel   17 ¾ x 38.7 c/m   12 x 11½ in.   Canvas   30.5 x 28.5 c/m

Cranach   'Judith'

Fouquet 'Louis XI'

Van Dyck   'Señor Miosa'

F. Clouet   'Louis de Nevers'

19½ x 13¾ in. Panel 49.5 x 35 c/m   14½ x 10¼ in. Panel 36 x 26 c/m   24 x 18¼ in. Panel. 61 x 46 c/m   9½ x 6¾ in. Panel 23¾ x 17 c/m

Romney   'Miss Mingay'

Th. Lawrence 'Miss Barnard'

R. V. der Weyden   'Young Man'

*Paintings Stolen from
the Brooklyn Museum
Brooklyn, N.Y.
May 1933*

15½ x 13½ in. Canvas 39.3 x 34.3 c/m 13½ x 10¾ Canvas 34½ x 27.3 c/m   6 x 5½ in. Panel   15 x 14 c/m

A view of the ten paintings stolen from the museum. Several are
now attributed to students of the old masters, not the masters
themselves.

While the police were still puzzling over the triple mystery, public interest lapsed. The curious crowds who came
to visit the scene of the crime stopped coming. The empty
frames were taken down, and the spaces filled with ten

museum was to be invulnerable—well, almost invulnerable, as time would prove.

Three months after the first robbery a second attempt was made. The fourth-floor gallery watchman spotted a shadowy intruder, sounded the alarm and gave chase. The would-be robber beat him down the stairs and escaped through an open window. All that the police could learn from the winded watchman was that the suspect was about twenty-five years old and toted a pistol.

Obviously the police had reason to wonder if there was a connection between incursions one and two. Was the second intruder a member of the same band? Or was he an amateur inspired by the success of the professionals? Whatever the answers were, it was embarrassing.

Just forty-eight hours later, the underworld was again guilty of contempt for the police. Once again, in the dead of night, there was somebody in the fourth-floor gallery for no good reason. His stealthy footsteps were overheard by an alert guard who tiptoed to a telephone to call the police. In answer, a hundred on- and off-duty police surrounded the building. But the quarry was as vigilant as the hunters. He got away without being seen. Once again, out of an open window. Once again, down a dangling rope—the same length and make of rope the thieves slid down in caper number one.

What could the men in blue do but suffer in silence and worry about the possibility of number four? And there was indeed going to be another robbery at the museum, but it wasn't to happen till long after Sweeney, Dugan, et al. had retired—not until 1974.

Fra Angelico   "Annunciation"

Rubens   "Christ's Ascension"

18 x 11 in.   Panel   35 x 28 c/m.

7 x 15¾ in.   Panel   17¾ x 35.7 c/m

12 x 11¾ in.   Canvas   30.5 x 29.5 c/m

F. Clouet   "Louis de Nevers"

Cranach   "Judith"

Fouquet "Louis XI"

Van Dyck   "Senor Miosa"

19¼ x 13¾ in. Panel 49.5 x 35 c/m

14¼ x 10¼in. Panel 36 x 26 c/m

24 x 18¼ in. Panel 61 x 46 c/m

9⅛ x 6¾ in. Panel 23¼ x 17 c/m

Romney   "Miss Mingay"

Th. Lawrence "Miss Barnard"

R. V. der Weyden   "Young Man"

*Paintings Stolen from
the Brooklyn Museum
Brooklyn, N.Y.
May 1933*

15¼ x 13½ in. Canvas 39.3 x 34.3 c/m

13¼ x 10¾ Canvas   34¼ x 27.3 c/m

6 x 5½ in. Panel   15 x 14 c/m

A view of the ten paintings stolen from the museum. Several are now attributed to students of the old masters, not the masters themselves.

While the police were still puzzling over the triple mystery, public interest lapsed. The curious crowds who came to visit the scene of the crime stopped coming. The empty frames were taken down, and the spaces filled with ten

62

other paintings of similar sizes from the museum's collection.

Then, two years after the original theft, the story broke into the press again. In the interim, Director Fox had been succeeded by his assistant, Philip N. Youtz. The new director let it be known that there was no need to look any farther than the museum storerooms for four of the pictures. He confessed that the quartet had been secretly hidden there shortly after they were reported stolen.

Yes, he admitted to newsmen, the museum had been deceiving the public, but it was a necessary deception, and the police were in on it. And so were the thieves.

The conspiracy of silence had been maintained for two years because each of the participants had a special self-interest in keeping mum. The museum wanted the paintings back. The police wanted the robbers. The robbers didn't want the police, but they seemed eager to restore the paintings to their rightful owner. Had they repented? Gone straight? Why else had they returned 40 percent of their ill-gotten gains?

Well, with all the crazy rule-breaking, there had been a method to their madness. They'd never intended to exert themselves unloading the loot. They had a ready-made buyer in mind all the time—the Brooklyn Museum.

Once Director Youtz made it clear that the robbery had been a kidnapping (such ventures came to be known as "artnappings"), the reappearance of the four canvases began to make sense. They'd been returned as proof that the ransom seekers held the other—far more valuable—six.

The gang was so well grounded in art that they knew

three of the pictures were only attributed to old masters. That is, art experts weren't certain whether the artists to whom they were credited had painted them. And the fourth, though not an "attributed to" work, was that of a lesser painter. These four, which were not in the same league money-wise as the others, were those that had been returned to the museum.

Youtz revealed that the museum had received a ransom note which offered to restore the four for free and set a low, quick turn-over sale price for the remaining six—thirty-eight thousand dollars. Like people kidnappers, the gang ordered the museum not to tell the police. Naturally, the museum told the police, who instructed them to pretend to follow the gang's instructions. Accordingly, a personal ad in the press had informed the crooks that they had a deal.

The gang's second note outlined the next steps. Enclosed was a key to a locker in Pennsylvania Station. Enclosed in the locker would be four paintings. If satisfied with paintings, Youtz should leave a package of thirty-eight thousand dollars over a specified newsstand in the Forty-second Street station of the IRT subway.

Key in hand, Youtz, shadowed unobtrusively by plainclothesmen, went to Pennsylvania Station. Pulses pounding, he opened the locker and extracted the canvases. There were four as promised. Indubitably they were the real articles. He could not help looking around for someone acting suspiciously. But in the crowd of commuters he saw no such person. Nor did the police.

So far, so good. All that remained, to recover the rest of

the plunder, was to follow the rest of the instructions.

Youtz did, except for two details: the bundle he put on the newsstand was a dummy, and it had been wired. The moment a finger was laid on it, lights would flash where the police had been staked out.

It was a very ingenious trap. The lawmen had the newsstand surrounded. The robbers couldn't possibly know the package was a phony, or wired, until they touched it. And then it would be too late.

The only trouble was that nobody ever fingered the bundle, or came anywhere near it.

The most reasonably obvious explanation for the no-show is that the gang had somehow gotten wise. But there is much in the annals of art theft that isn't reasonable or obvious. A thief has been known to take a masterpiece for profit, and then become so enamored of it that he wouldn't part with it for any sum of money. This sort of eccentricity may not make much sense to anyone but a true art-appreciator. For that matter only real connoisseurs of art have any business in the stealing end of it.

When you come right down to it the legitimate inhabitants of the art world operate under equally unpredictable rules. What makes one oil-covered canvas priceless, and another not worth the canvas it's painted on? If it's the judgment of the critics that makes a masterpiece, then how come so many authenticated masterpieces turn out to be forgeries? If the acknowledged experts are so expert, why is it that so many have so often been wrong in evaluating the work of new artists? What kind of know-how is it that makes it impossible for a work to be given away—a painting that later costs more than most millionaires can afford?

The fact is that art, like beauty of all kinds, is in the eye of the beholder. And unless you're in the art trade as a dealer or collector, curator or crook, you don't have to know anything about art to know what you like to look at.

The reason it took Director Youtz two years to come clean with press and public was that he had been trying desperately to resume negotiations with the gang. There were ads pleading for forgiveness, pledging to deal this time in good faith. But there'd been no peep out of the kidnappers. His confession was an admission that he'd given up hope. Thus, the curtain came down on an unhappy ending to the 1933 occurrences at the Brooklyn Museum.

It took a long time before the police came to the museum again. To be precise, forty-one years and seven months from the time a rope was dangled out of a window.

Art-crook history repeated itself on December 31, 1974. Michael Botwinick, who had become director of the Brooklyn Museum, informed the police that somebody had somehow walked off with master painter Auguste Renoir's *Still Life With Blue Cup*—a small, easily transportable, one-of-a-kind work of French impressionism, valued at fifty thousand dollars.

Back in '33, Director Fox, harassed by misfortune, plagued by reporters about his less than tight security, defended himself thus: "Anything out of the ordinary is not agreeable. But no institution run by human beings is infallible." Botwinick would have had to agree. With modern burglar-proof alarm systems, and with all the most up-to-date security measures, the Brooklyn Museum was yet human. So humanly fallible, in fact, that Botwinick had never even heard of the first robbery. Apparently, as successive generations of directors handed over the reins, word of the missing masterpieces was not passed along.

Of course, in 1974 things were different. There was a new generation of policemen, and (one must assume) a new generation of robbers. There was no rope clue, no open window. And if there was a ransom note, it has been kept secret.

But the more some things change, the more they remain the same. Like the first time, there were no prints, no suspects. Current art-theft expert Detective Robert Volpe alerted the United States Customs Service, as had his predecessor, and added Interpol and the FBI. Photographs of the missing Renoir were sent to authorities abroad and at home. No one could predict what luck Volpe would have. But in some high art circles there was considerable optimism, judging by an announcement in the *New York Times:* "To fill the Brooklyn's temporary gap, the Metropolitan Museum of Art has lent it the artist's *The Bay of Naples* until the stolen work is recovered."

As time passed, the "temporary gap" began to look as permanent as the gaps left on the museum walls by the theft two score years before. Then, nineteen months after the Renoir vanished, the case took a startling turn. A six-by-thirteen-inch package wrapped in plain brown paper, addressed to Director Michael Botwinick, arrived in the mail. Botwinick's secretary removed the paper wrapping only to find a second layer of plastic, and then a third, a pillow case, and under that still another of white tissue

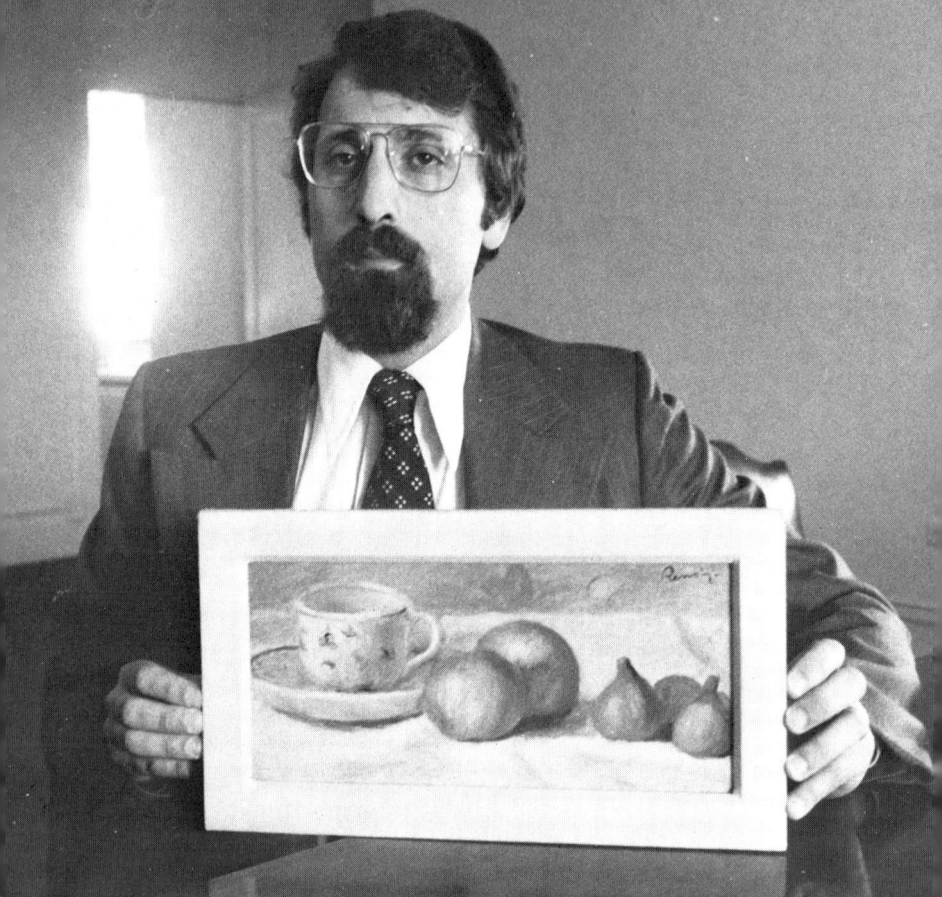

Director Michael Botwinick with the contents of his surprise
package—Renoir's *Still Life with Blue Cup*.

paper. It was only after she peeled off the tissue that she
discovered the parcel wasn't a practical joke. There, taped
to a thin board, was the missing *Still Life with Blue Cup*—

the real, genuine fifty-thousand-dollar painting, unabraded, unscratched, unscarred, in exactly the same condition it had been in when it was stolen.

The case became curiouser and curiouser. When Botwinick examined the wrappings for a clue to the identity of the anonymous benefactor, he found some helpful hints scrawled in red ink on the reverse side of the brown paper: "The museums in the United States need armed guards it won't be long before armed robberys of art museums are happening and believe me I know!"

This presumably well-meant advice or ill-meant warning did not impel Director Botwinick to distribute precautionary shotguns to his men. "We change security at regular and unplanned intervals," he told the press, "and every time we change security we strengthen it."

Detective Volpe found other clues on the brown paper: a metered mail stamp which proved that the packager had invested eighty-two cents in a post office somewhere in Brooklyn, and—most unusual—a return address, that of an existing building. But trying to track down the thief through the postage meter stamp didn't get anywhere, and Volpe soon came to the conclusion that none of the inhabitants at the return address had posted the parcel.

With all his expertise in art thefts, Detective Volpe found himself unable to fathom the motive behind the return of the painting or the reason for the warning. Nevertheless he was thinking positively. "The theft has some meaning now," he told reporters. "The fact that it returned in this manner with a note gives us some direction to go in."

Exactly what meaning he had in mind, and what direction it gave him, is still to be revealed—perhaps when the thief and/or the parcel poster are found. Three days after the postman had delivered *Still Life with Blue Cup,* the canvas was once again filling the gap on the fifth floor of the museum—permanently, it is hoped.

THE MAN WITH THE MONKEY NOSE:
The Kidnapping of Charley Ross

•

WHEN THE BURGLAR alarm clanged in Holmes Van Brunt's Long Island mansion on December 17, 1874, he woke with a start, swore at the prospect of going out into the predawn storm, and sleepily groped for his pants. He hadn't the remotest idea that he was about to bring to an end the search for the criminals responsible for the first kidnapping in America.

All that he knew was that something, wind or rain, or someone had tripped the warning system in his brother's shuttered summer home, and he'd better take a looksee. He roused his son, his gardener and his hired man, and though he was almost certain that a short circuit had set off the bells, he took precautions. Armed with shotguns and pistols, the four men went reluctantly out into the freezing blackness of the December downpour to investigate.

As they slogged toward the adjacent house, they saw the faint beams of two lanterns moving through the empty rooms. They cocked their weapons and prepared to ambush the robbers when they emerged with their loot. But the housebreakers were doing a thorough, leisurely job. Time passed and the watchers got wetter and colder, and so impatient that they decided to enter the house. They were heard. The lanterns went out. The intruders ran. They were met by a fusillade of gunfire.

The shooting stopped when both of the robbers were down. One was dead. The other, a younger man, was bleeding from many wounds. Told by Van Brunt that he was dying, he gasped that he was Joe Douglas, his dead companion was Bill Mosher, and that together they had kidnapped little Charley Ross. Before he could say any more, he was dead.

Headlines shouted that the kidnapping of July 1, 1874, had finally been solved. Though everyone was certain these were the wanted men, witnesses were brought to the morgue to view the corpses. The only eyewitness to the actual crime was a six-year-old boy, Charley's brother, Walter. Never having looked at death before, Walter was terrified. But he manfully identified Mosher, whom he had described as "monkey nose," and Douglas as the two who took him and his little brother for a ride to buy firecrackers.

It is at least questionable whether a judge and jury would have found Mosher and Douglas guilty, since the case against them rested so heavily on the testimony of a child. But even if they were the kidnappers, the mystery was not solved by their deaths, for Charley Ross was never found.

The case of four-year-old Charles Brewster Ross was a tragedy of errors from the very beginning: mistakes made by the good people from the best of motives, mistakes made by the bad people from the worst of motives. The trouble was that neither the law nor the lawbreakers had had any experience with this sort of crime. Never before in America had a child been held for ransom.

Those were innocent years, the 1880s. Of course there were crimes of passion and for profit. And there were instances of Fagins who spirited children away and taught them the thief trade. There were tales of wandering Gypsies who stole children to adopt into their tribes. But these were slum children. Not much fuss was ever made about their disappearance.

Charley Ross, however, was an upper-middle-class boy. He was taken from an elite section of Philadelphia. His father, Christian K. Ross, was a very substantial citizen, a prominent merchant, from one of Philadelphia's first families. The Rosses' economic and social position was key to the case—for their peers reasoned that if it could happen to the Rosses, it could happen to them. That had to be prevented at all costs.

Kidnapping was so inconceivable to Ross, as it would be to the rest of his class, that until the ransom note was received, three days after the boy disappeared, he believed Charley had just strayed away. A reward was offered for "a lost small boy with long curly flaxen hair, hazel eyes, round face, dressed in a brown linen suit with short skirt, broad brimmed hat and laced shoes."

The police assumption that Charley was lost seems naive even for those unsophisticated days. Walter had told them that two nice men, one with a monkey nose, had taken him and Charley for a ride in a horse and buggy. The men had dropped Walter off with a quarter in his hand to buy fireworks in a cigar store while they waited for him. Walter said that when he came out with his purchase, the two nice men and his brother were gone. He looked all over for the buggy, couldn't find it anywhere, and started to cry. The story was continued by a passerby who saw the weeping child and returned him to his home. Ross had been scouring the neighborhood in search of his missing sons.

In the opinion of the police, the two men had taken the boys for a jaunt in an excess of pre-Fourth of July alcoholic high spirits. They calmed the distracted Ross by assuring him that as soon as the merrymakers sobered up they would return Charley with shamefaced apologies. By the second day the drunken lark theory was supplemented by a hypothesis that the men had been ashamed to return Charley and had let him off somewhere, and he was being kept by some citizen who would want recompense for returning him. The police urged Ross to relax. The offer of a reward would bring Charley home.

While Ross was trying to be patient, Dr. Walker, a Germantown physician, confirmed Walter's description of the two men. He reported that on his rounds he had seen two men in a buggy parked near the Ross house. He hadn't paid too much attention, but he had noticed that the older man had a somewhat deformed nose. Till then the police had not paid much attention to Walter's "man with a monkey nose."

Walker's information that the men had been casing the premises made the police junk their previous theories. Yet they could think of no reason for the men to have taken the boy, except perhaps that Ross had some enemy who wanted to make trouble for him. But try as hard as he could, Ross could think of no one whom he could have given any reason to take his son.

Then on July Fourth the first ransom note came. It was the beginning of a correspondence that marked a new era in crime. Ross and the police read it unbelievingly. No one had ever received or for that matter written such a letter before. It said:

> July 3. Mr. Ros be not uneasy you son charly bruster be al writ we is got him and no powers on earth can deliver out of our hand—you wil hav two pay us befor you git him from us an pay us a big cent to—if you put the cops hunting for him you is only defeeting yu own end we is got him fix so no living power can gits him from us alive if any aproch is maid to his hidin place that is the signil for his instant anihilation—if yu regard his lif puts no one to search for him you money can fech him out alive an no other existin powers don't deceve yuself and think the detectives can hid him from us for that is one imposebel you here from us in a few day

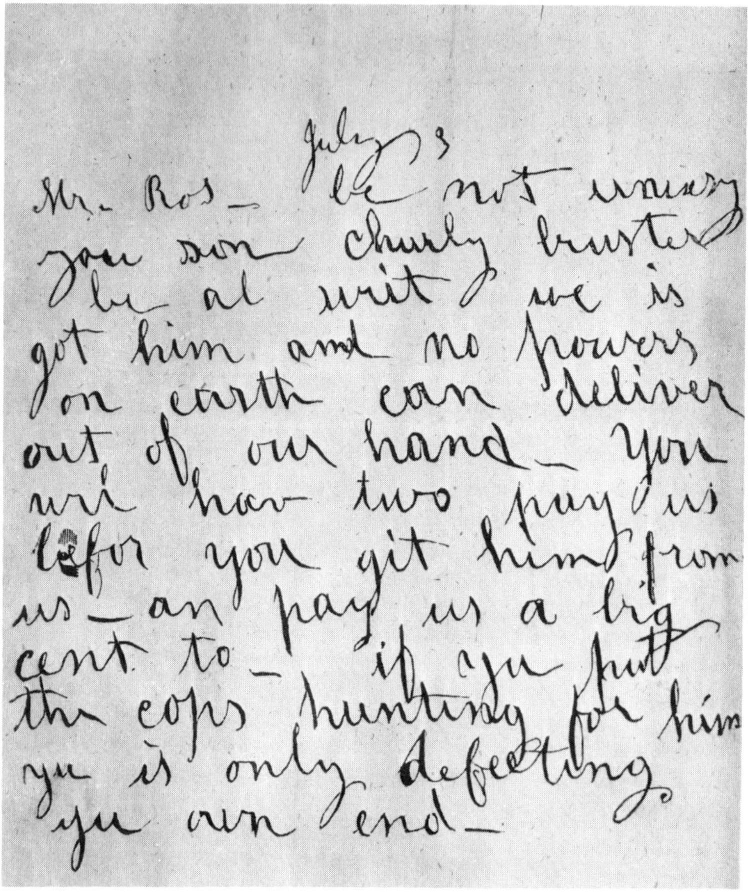

The ransom note of July 3.

There it was in black and white. Inconceivable, unprecedented, monstrous. Christian Ross reacted to the illiterate scrawl as any father would. He read the letter in fear for his son's life. He wanted him back no matter what.

The police responded differently. They saw the ransom demand as a threat, not only against little Charley but against all children of moneyed parents. If it were paid, no child would be safe. Paramount in their minds was catching and punishing the criminals. Of course, it was implicit that when they found the criminals they would also find Charley.

As a good citizen, Christian Ross had to go along. He had already, though innocently, ignored the note's warning against involving the police. Though he took the threat of Charley's "instant anihilation" to heart, he was a pillar of Philadelphia society, and he saw justice in the police approach. He could not let his individual self-interest take precedence over the general interest of his peers.

Besides, the police were certain to find his boy. They had ordered the most intensive search of the city ever conducted. Ferries, depots, barns, stables; any remotely suspicious person, place, vehicle would be investigated. In the light of this dragnet, it seemed that the kidnappers' boast, "no living power can gits him from us alive," was ridiculous. The odds against the malefactors were tremendous. Hundreds of policemen in uniform, detectives in civilian dress, aroused citizens of Philadelphia were hunting for them. At the very least they would be forced to release the child.

But the strenuous day-and-night effort of the police and

their allies got nowhere. Some people were beginning to believe the kidnappers would never be heard from again when, on July 8, a second note was delivered to Ross's store downtown. The price for the return of Charley was "20000 not one doler lest."

It is entirely possible that if Ross had had the money, he would have paid the ransom despite the police. But although the criminals had taken the child of a prominent, presumably affluent merchant, Ross did not have twenty thousand dollars or anything like it. The depression of 1873 had struck him severely. He was in debt, close to bankruptcy, and his elaborate home was an attempt to keep up appearances.

The police reasoned that if the kidnappers understood that no money would be given them, they would let the boy go. The flaw in this reasoning for Ross was a statement in the second letter: "if yu love money more than child yu be its murderer not us for the money we will heve if we don't get from yu we be sure to get it from someone els for we wil make example of yure child that others may be wiser."

The threat to make an example of Charley, so that other parents would pay future demands, only strengthened the authorities' conviction that the ransom should not be paid. They were still confident that they would apprehend the criminals and rescue the child. Though Ross was much less confident, he had to go along.

In accord with the strategy worked out between the police and a committee of city leaders, Ross followed the second letter's instructions. He inserted an ad in the *Philadel-*

phia Ledger which appeared the following morning: "Ros we be ready to negotiate."

Of course the strategists had no intention of negotiating. They were playing for time. While they were waiting to hear from the kidnappers, they intensified their efforts to find them. So sure were the law enforcers that they'd lay hands on the criminals that they made no attempt to conceal their duplicity. The wanted men read the dragnet stories in the press, and saw the posters which were prominently displayed in New York as well as in Philadelphia, but they were willing to continue to parley.

In note #3 they wrote Ross: "use the detectives as yu pleas but dont let them mislede yu to the sacrifice of Charley."

The committee read this as a sign that the kidnappers' original threats against the boy's life were not to be taken seriously. But try as he could to be reasonable, Christian Ross was increasingly frightened. His efforts to reassure his wife, Sarah, that everything would be all right failed because he himself didn't believe it. And so for the first time in his life he rebelled against the establishment he had unfailingly supported.

The object of the next meeting between Ross and the committee was to decide how to respond to the third note. It demanded that an ad be placed in which Ross would say "Ros wil come to terms" or "Ros wil not come to terms."

Ross told the committee that he had decided to come to terms; that he was going to borrow the twenty thousand dollars ransom and get his son back. But now he ran into the committee's stern warning that if he did he would be compounding a felony. That was the law. For a man like Ross, to whom respect for law and order was as natural as breathing, this information was shattering. He could defy the counsel of his peers and the police, but not the immutable law.

With a heavy heart he surrendered to the dictates of the meeting. The personal he ran in the press in answer to note #3 hedged: "Ros will come to terms to the extent of his ability."

The kidnapping was a sensational, front page, continued story in the newspapers. The missing child's parents were hounded by reporters who ferreted out Ross's abortive rebellion against the authorities. Editorials in New York and Philadelphia took an outraged, vehement stand on the side of law and order. The ransom must not be paid. The criminals would not dare to harm Charley. Ross must put himself entirely in the hands of the police who would certainly catch the criminals.

Though Ross dutifully followed the directives of the authorities, he also continued to make secret efforts to borrow the twenty thousand dollars among his friends.

The police followed up clues that poured in from well-meaning citizens. Gypsies, tramps, suspicious-looking members of the so-called criminal classes were arrested, interrogated, then released. The procedures the police were following were standard, tested, proved by their experience in dealing with crime. But this was the first case of its kind, and their years of accumulated know-how did not work. In regard to kidnapping, they were amateurs.

But for that matter this was a first for the criminals, too.

Charley Ross.

They were also amateurs: they continued to negotiate, thus allowing the delay to continue, and making their capture more likely.

That the kidnappers were aware of their danger was made clear in their fourth letter: "is it necessary to repeat the fatle consequences of delaying to give time to detectives to find his hidin place." But they set no time limit. Instead, they put it up to Ross. They asked, "how much time yu want to obtain this money." And, extraordinarily, they spoke as reasonable businessmen to a fellow businessman, making a deal. "Ros this undertaken cost us $1000 to prepare the machinery to perform the work." This has the sound of a salesman defending the price of his goods. As the correspondence progressed, the writers were gradually abandoning the carefully feigned illiteracy of the first note.

On the ninth day following Charley's disappearance, Ross, in ever deepening despair, qualified the reply to letter #4. He had been told to advertise, "Ros i is got it and be wilin to pay it." Though he took literally the blunt threat, "we want no other anser and on the fath of yu word his lif hang," he consented to the police decision to respond: "Ros is wiling; have not got it; am doing my best to raise it."

Until this fourth interchange of correspondence, the kidnappers had replied to each ad within hours. But now a day passed, then another, without word. Charley's parents had to believe that the criminals had carried out their repeated threats to kill the boy. By Sunday, July 12, the third day of silence, the police were sufficiently alarmed to feel that a change in tactics was necessary. The personal ad they prepared followed the abductors' instructions to the letter: "Ros I is got it and be wilin to pay it."

Whatever hope Christian and Sarah Ross had for the return of their son began to vanish as no word was received from the kidnappers. Neither would admit it to the other but both were in reality mourning their son. But then, once again, their hopes were renewed by the receipt of note #5.

This time Ross was ordered: "have the $20,000 in denomination not exceeding 'tens' have yu money were yu can git it any moment wen cal for . . ." To convince him that he would indeed have Charley at home "in 5 ours after we receive the mony and find it correct," they argued: "After we gets the mony we has no further use for the child, and it is to our interest then to restor him home unharmed, so that others will rely on our word."

The police and citizens' committee pounced on the writers' stated self-interest in returning the boy unharmed once they had the ransom. Although they had not taken the threats to Charley's life seriously, they now took in earnest the criminals' expressed intent to build a kidnapping business. It proved that payment of the ransom would guarantee other children would be kidnapped.

Clearly this could not be allowed. The committee increased the pressure on Ross, knowing how desperately he wanted to buy back his son. At home he had to face the accusation of Charley's empty bed, and the unspoken question, "When are you going to bring Charley home?" Tormented by his sense of inadequacy as a father, he could only repeat the reassurances impressed upon him at his meetings with the authorities, but they sounded hollow to him, and he knew Sarah had no faith in them.

For his wife there was no conflict, no wavering, no indecision. No matter what the cost, or what rules were broken, no matter what anyone thought, she wanted her son, quickly. She listened dutifully to her husband's explanations of strategy and tactics, but they had no effect on her. Of course, she was not asked to the meetings. A good wife of her time and position could not quarrel with the decisions of her husband. She had promised. She kept her promise. The only signs of her disobedience were her dreadful misery and the loss of her physical health.

Now that he knew the terms, Ross was at a crucial turning point. The money was not a problem any longer. He could have borrowed it from his wife's family. Indeed, a complete stranger had offered to give it to him. But he was still a prisoner of his upper-middle-class upbringing, still committed to belonging. Even so, the committee did not trust him not to deal with the kidnappers.

He had to consent to a twenty-four-hour tail by plainclothesmen, the new plan to entrap the criminals, although he'd been warned "any fals act on yu part seals the fate of yu child and closes any further bisniss with us." His next ad was the ultimate false act. "Ros. It is redy. You have my word for it." But nobody ever came for the supposedly ready twenty thousand dollars.

During the two weeks Charley had been absent, the five anonymous letters had been mailed from the Philadelphia main post office, despite a police watch. But following a story in the *Philadelphia Inquirer* which revealed that the post office was under surveillance, the police demanded a news blackout. Some papers attacked this attempt "to muzzle the free press," adding nasty comments about police ineffectiveness, bungling and stupidity.

As a result of the police and press name-calling a valuable lead was lost. The sixth ransom letter was mailed at a street post office box in Philadelphia. This communication was an apology. The reason the ransom had not been called for was: "we had to go a bit out in the country an the blasted old orse give out so we could not get back in time." They swore, "may our blasted sols be eternaly damed if we do not keep our word." They warned again not to let the detectives know they were coming for the money, which was to be put in a "smal strong ruf box" and made available at a minute's notice.

Message #6 revealed a thoughtful analysis of the social forces involved in the affair. "let yu friends advise yu," the writer pleaded, "not the detectives they study their own interest and the interest of society yu have a duty to perform to yourself that stands paramount to all else in the world . . ."

The letter was received on Thursday, July 16. It set Saturday the twentieth as the day the abductors would be ready to exchange boy for money. The police assumed not only that the criminals were simple-minded, but that they would not carry out their threat to destroy the child. They staked out the Ross house, planning to trail whoever came for the money, and in one swoop arrest criminals and recover Charley.

From Friday night until Sunday morning Sarah and

Christian Ross waited for a knock on their door. Keeping vigil with them, in hiding places, were detectives. Hour after hour passed in tense, expectant silence. But no messenger came.

It turned out that the kidnappers had not kept the rendezvous because they had been reading the newspapers. In their next letter, they accused Ross of double-dealing: "Ros: we be at a loss to understand yu a week ago yu sed yu had the amont an was wilin to pay it the editorials seme to speak as if the mony was yet to be contributed befor yu could pay it." They recognized the mistake they had made in assuming he was as affluent as the circumstances of his life indicated. But there was no turning back. "we thought yu were better fixt for money or we would never took yu child but since we have him we shal cary out our plan with him." Despite all, they were still willing to deal, but "dont yu state in personals that yu have the mony until yu have it naled up in the box an redy to give wen caled for."

In response to the public outcry for action the police made an arrest. The suspect, named Wooster, was a glib, fast-talking swindler with a long record. The evidence against him was a similarity between his penmanship and that of the ransom notes.

Wooster claimed he was innocent. He defended himself by maintaining that there were easier ways of making a stake than stealing kids. The kidnappers took time to let it be known (in another note) that Wooster was telling the truth. After a week, during which the press tried him, found him guilty at first, and then absolved him, Wooster was reluctantly released by the police.

Interviewed by the *New York Herald* when he was freed, Wooster editorialized about the case from the point of view of a professional criminal. He was convinced that the boy would not be returned unless the ransom was paid—the whole twenty thousand dollars.

Why? "What would you reckon as fair compensation for giving up home and being in exile for the rest of your life?" he reasoned. "The publicity had made Philadelphia uninhabitable for the abductors." Is twenty thousand dollars too much when you are debarred from such rich, gullible cities as Philadelphia, guarded by such an idiotic police force? This professional estimate of police inadequacy from the other side of the law was seconded by many law-abiding citizens.

Press criticism of the police mounted as some of the reporters began to do their own detecting. They found many loopholes in the nets the police had cast and other promising leads the police had overlooked, but nothing came of them.

When the press urged that the city of Philadelphia offer a reward for the return of the child, Philadelphia's Mayor Stokeley responded with an absolute refusal. He compared the kidnapping to stealing property. "When goods are stolen I don't wish them returned so much as I wish those who stole them brought to justice," he declared. The issue was never more bluntly stated. He went further: "If anyone on the force turns up stolen goods without bringing the thief to prison, the officer will be discharged."

Mayor Stokeley's attitude seems outrageous today. But in the America of that day, when the priority of property rights over human rights was largely unchallenged, it was very reasonable. The mayor was only voicing the belief of his propertied constituency. It was appalling to Christian Ross that his son was thought of as "stolen goods," but he was a member of that constituency, and he could not yet free himself from the values of his peers.

Of course, the kidnappers read the mayor's pronouncement. They read as well an interview with Christian Ross in which he said: "I place no confidence in these men and shall not do as they request." And the reverse: "Thus far I have no fears for the child's safety. All the letters assure me the child is safe and in good health." And, reversing himself again, "My greatest apprehension is that, finding they do not get the money, the child may suffer for it."

Not "my child," but "the child." Odd for a father to refer to his son in such a manner. How, after pledging to negotiate and accept their terms, could he say he never had any intention of dealing with them? Does his contradictory statement, widely reprinted, make sense? If he had no confidence in the men, why did he accept their statement that the boy was safe? And if his non-confidence in their threats was true, why then did he have apprehensions for the boy's life if the money were not paid?

Obviously this letter, composed during the meeting between authority and Ross, reflects Ross's real feeling only in part. No one knows how much he struggled against the committee. Regardless of what he felt, his statement told the kidnappers he was confident they would return the boy when they finally realized that the ransom would never be paid.

It may be that Ross was led to agree to defy the criminals. On July 22, the next day, handbills were distributed throughout the city offering:

$20,000 REWARD FOR THE KIDNAPPERS

The money had been contributed by bankers and other men of means meeting with Mayor Stokely. It was to be paid "for the arrest and conviction of the abductors of CHARLES BREWSTER ROSS . . . and the restoration of the child to his parents." In that order. The offer was accompanied by a description of the two men and the boy. Somehow, inexplicably, it neglected to mention the older man's grotesque "monkey nose."

The nationally circulated reward offer produced a spate of Charley Rosses and arrests all over the country. But it left the mystery still unsolved.

Evidently convinced that the kidnappers were imbeciles and had not read Ross's widely printed refusal to negotiate, the authorities bought another personal ad. It said: "Money is ready. How shall I know your agent?"

Logically there was no earthly reason to expect any response to this obviously phony communication. Yet there was a logic to the answer mailed in Camden, New Jersey. The writer noted the conflict between Ross's statement of no confidence and the "money is ready" ad: "nevertheless we wil act upon yu promise as if it was made by an angle." This was because, "from the nature of this bisiness it is to be presumed neither can have implicit confidence." It reiterated that once they had the ransom they would have no further use for Charley and would return him. And it added a postscript about identifying their agent: "we wil send prof with him so yu can no him when he comes."

Ross's personal ad on July 22 agreed to comply in every particular. It was answered by a strange note on July 24, which announced a week's delay because "our creed is such it forbids us to do any bisiness of this kind only at a certain quarter of the moon." This may be the only known instance of criminals being astrologically guided. Perhaps the police would have been more successful if they too had looked to the zodiac for leadership.

The writer regretted the postponement: "this delay may be a great sorce of torture to yu but it cannot be avoided." It is extremely unlikely that the bereaved parents could find a satisfactory answer to the abductors' question, "why do they not pay their mony to have yours restored first an then offer a reward for our conviction?"

The Ross family continued to be deluged with advice, suggestions, correspondence. Their home was invaded by crackpots of all kinds: publicity seekers, religious fanatics, mediums with clues from the other world, con men hoping to latch onto a fast buck, inquiring reporters in various disguises and well-intentioned sympathizers with offers of money.

The sensation-seeking press, lacking scoops, made them up. In this heyday of yellow journalism, any rumor, innuendo or character assassination was fit to print. Headlined were anonymous letters which cast suspicion on Mr. and Mrs. Ross and even Walter as accomplices in the crime. The press pointed to Ross's need of money, suggested that Charley was buried on the Ross property, talked of skeletons in the family closet which had caused Ross to spirit the boy away, charged that the anonymous letters were written by Ross himself. Ultimately Ross brought a libel suit against the *Philadelphia Eagle* which had called the kidnapping a fraud. The paper was fined. But the libels didn't cease.

When the moon turned to the favorable phase desired by the kidnappers, on July 28, they wrote Ross to have the money ready by the thirtieth. More detectives were added to the detail concealed in and around the Ross home, prepared for the visitor on the thirtieth.

On the thirtieth no visitor came. Instead there arrived a letter detailing a foolproof scheme to avoid entrapment. It ordered Ross to journey by train that very afternoon to New York City and thence to Albany. Somewhere along this route he would be given a signal, a bell and white flag by day, a torch and flag by night. He was told to stand on the rear platform of the train. When he saw the signal, he was to throw out a valise with the ransom. But if the train was stopped and the signaler arrested, "you child's fate is sealed." And finally if contact had not been made when Ross reached Albany, he would find a letter in the Albany post office directing him where to continue his journey.

This letter was different from all the others. There was no attempt to negotiate, nor to persuade, to point out the mistakes Ross was making. Most ominous to Ross was the final sentence: "this letter ends all things in regard to the restoration of yu child."

Another meeting decided that Ross was to go on the journey as directed, except that he would be accompanied by his nephew and a plainclothesman, and instead of the money, the valise would contain a letter. It was composed by the committee, signed by Ross, and it insisted, "I cannot throw away twenty thousand dollars on the wild plan you suggested." It proposed a simultaneous exchange—money for boy.

Valise in hand, Ross stood on the rear platform of the train from Philadelphia to New York, his eyes straining for the signal that might come any place along the way. There was none. The detective trailed him through Grand Central Station in New York to the rear platform post on the Albany train. No torch lit up the gathering darkness. Nor was there the promised letter in the Albany post office. Ross stayed over in Albany. Perhaps the letter had been delayed. But no letter arrived.

What had gone wrong? What had prevented the criminals from going through with their plan? Had they changed their minds? The explanation was received at Ross's place of business during his absence. On July 30 newspaper extras proclaimed that Charley Ross had been found in the town of Hamburg, seventy-five miles from Philadelphia, and that Ross had gone there to claim his boy.

Accordingly the kidnappers had concluded Ross was still not convinced that only they had Charley, and only they could return him. Naturally, they'd called off their agent. They were now giving him a last chance. His intentions should be made known in a personal ad addressed to John.

On August 2, thirty-two days after the search for Charley had begun, Ross advertised, "Your directions were followed. You did not keep faith. Point out some sure and less public way of communicating either by letter or person."

In the next day's letter the criminals acknowledged their mistake. They told Ross to have the money in the box, ready in his store. They went so far as to promise, "if we lose our money through our agent yu get yu child just as if we got every dollar."

Taking the criminals' continuance of negotiations as a sign of their weakness, the authorities took a hard line. Ross answered, "Propositions are impossible. Action must be simultaneous." On August 4 the criminals wrote, "We shal not communicate with yu any more unles yu want to redeem yu child on our terms." They left one way out for Ross: "if you have anything to say to us it must be through the personals of the *New York Herald*." Clearly they were matching the hard line of the police.

The police got even tougher. They completely ignored the note for the next three weeks. During this time both sides clung to their immovable positions. Contact was broken.

The action of the drama shifted to New York in September when a convicted horse thief and burglar, Gil Mosher, accused his fifty-two-year-old brother, William, of being the kidnapper. He told New York Police Superintendent George Walling that his brother Bill had once proposed they kidnap one of Commodore Vanderbilt's grandchildren with a plan identical to that of the Ross abduction. He went on to implicate Bill's partner, a younger man, Joe Douglas, and as a clincher he produced examples of Bill's handwriting which the police decided was similar to that of the ransom notes.

From this point on, the police were convinced that Bill

Mosher and Joe Douglas were the men they were looking for, though Gil's credibility as a witness was less than solid. They knew he wanted to revenge himself on his brother for having cheated him out of the proceeds of a robbery, and that he would sell his mother for the reward or any part of it. Yet his information was as close as they had come to any break in the case.

As soon as Mosher was accused, a New York detective who had once arrested Bill Mosher remembered that his prisoner had a deformed nose, which made him fit little Walter Ross's description, "the man with the monkey nose."

Now a national search for Bill Mosher and Joe Douglas was launched. And because the New York police knew Bill was a devoted husband and father who could be expected to be in touch with his family, a hunt was ordered for his wife, Martha, and her four children. Martha and her kids should have been easier to locate than the wanted men, but they weren't.

In his eagerness for the reward, Gil gave the police another lead. He pointed them at Martha's brother, William Westervelt, a former policeman discharged from the force for covering up a gambling ring, part-time horsecar conductor and bosom buddy of Bill Mosher. Westervelt was picked up and held till little Walter Ross could be brought from Philadelphia to take a look at him. The boy was certain that he was not one of the men who had taken him and Charley for a ride.

Usually when a suspect of less than blameless character is cleared, he tends to put as much distance as possible be-

tween himself and the police. Not Westervelt. He had some fish he wanted New York's finest to fry for him.

Of all the extraordinary circumstances in this case, the police connection with Westervelt was to prove the most bizarre. From moment to moment he changed from stool pigeon to his brother-in-law's keeper, and back again. During the months the New York police believed they were manipulating him, he was manipulating the police. When he was caught in a lie, or his double dealing was exposed, Westervelt always admitted it, always had a persuasive explanation.

The relationship with Westervelt, during which the trail got alternately hot and cold, was kept top secret. Christian Ross had no part in it. It was all out of his hands. All he was allowed to do was take instructions and check out the increasing number of "Charley Rosses" that kept being found after a group of eminent Philadelphians hired the Pinkertons, America's most famous eyes. These sleuths distributed millions of circulars which turned up Charleys in almost every state, and in Canada and Cuba.

When the New York police saw fit they reported their progress to the Philadelphia police, who in their turn reported to Ross what they thought he should know. It may be that the less he was told about the frustrating twists and turns the New York inquiry took at Westervelt's direction, the better off he was.

The head man in New York, Police Superintendent George Walling, dealt personally with Westervelt, the closest they had come to the kidnappers. Unlike the ordinary informer who wants cash for his wares, Westervelt

$20,000 REWARD

Has been offered for the recovery of CHARLIE BREWSTER ROSS, and for the arrest and conviction of his abductors. He was stolen from his parents in Germantown, Pa., on July 1st, 1874, by two unknown men.

DESCRIPTION OF THE CHILD.

The accompanying portrait resembles the child, but is not a correct likeness. He is about four years old; his body and limbs are straight and well formed; he has a round, full face; small chin, with noticeable dimple; very regular and pretty dimpled hands; small, well-formed neck; full, broad forehead; bright dark-brown eyes, with considerable fullness over them; clear white skin; healthy complexion; light flaxen hair, of silky texture, easily curled in ringlets when it extends to the neck; hair darker at the roots,—slight cowlick on left side where parted; very light eyebrows. He talks plainly, but is retiring, and has a habit of putting his arm up to his eyes when approached by strangers. His skin may now be stained, and hair dyed,—or he may be dressed as a girl, with hair parted in the centre.

DESCRIPTION OF THE KIDNAPPERS.

No. 1 is about thirty-five years old; five feet nine inches high; medium build, weighing about one hundred and fifty pounds; rather full, round face, florid across the nose and cheek-bones, giving him the appearance of a hard drinker; he had sandy moustache, but was otherwise clean shaved; wore eye-glasses, and had an open-faced gold watch and gold vest-chain; also, green sleeve-buttons.

No. 2 is older, probably about forty years of age, and a little shorter and stouter than his companion; he wore chin whiskers about three inches long, of a reddish-sandy color; and had a pug-nose, or a nose in some way deformed. He wore gold bowed spectacles, and had two gold rings on one of his middle fingers, one plain and one set with red stone.

Both men wore brown straw hats, one high- and one low-crowned; one wore a linen duster; and, it is thought, one had a duster of gray alpaca, or mohair.

Any person who shall discover or know of any child, which there is reason to believe may be the one abducted, will at once communicate with their Chief of Police or Sheriff, who has been furnished with means for the identification of the stolen child.

Otherwise, communications by letter or telegraph, if necessary, will be directed to either of the following officers of

PINKERTON'S NATIONAL DETECTIVE AGENCY.

Viz.:

BENJ. FRANKLIN, Sup't, 45 S. Third St., Philadelphia, Pa.
R. A. PINKERTON, Sup't, 66 Exchange Place, New York.
F. WARNER, Sup't, 191 and 193 Fifth Avenue, Chicago, Ill.
GEO. H. BANGS, Gen'l Sup't.

ALLAN PINKERTON.

PHILADELPHIA, *August 22d*, 1874.

(POST THIS UP IN A CONSPICUOUS PLACE.)

The Pinkerton Agency circular.

wanted to be paid in services. In return for letting Walling know when he next heard from Mosher, Westervelt wanted the superintendent to get him full-time employment from the horsecar company and/or reinstatement in the police department. His third condition was that his co-operation with the police remain secret. Walling agreed to everything.

When Walling was getting nowhere with the horsecar owners or the police board, Westervelt put on some pressure. It took an emotional turn. He could not in all decency finger his brother-in-law because it would be so terrible for his poor innocent sister and her little ones. Walling was very understanding. Blood, he agreed, was much thicker than water. It would be inhuman to expect Westervelt to betray Mosher. All Westervelt need do was lead him to Douglas. Westervelt was vastly relieved by the superintendent's display of compassion.

Who was kidding whom? If the policeman thought the informer was too dumb to realize that Douglas would lead to Mosher, he was mistaken. In this game of wits he was outmatched. Walling was to learn that his trickiness would work against him.

Westervelt insisted that though he was in his brother-in-law's confidence, he had never heard him mention a word about kidnapping Charley Ross or anyone else. He also swore from his knowledge of Mosher it was impossible for him to have stolen a child. Having thus told the police

97

what they did not want to hear, Westervelt smoothly reversed himself. He managed to remember that in June, only weeks before Charley was stolen, Bill had proudly shown him a horse and buggy he had just bought. Walling dug out a composite drawing of the kidnap buggy, made from the description of witnesses. Westervelt studied it carefully and said that, except for some minor details, it mirrored the one Mosher had bought.

Splendid. Here was more evidence against Mosher. Obviously, Westervelt was the key to the case—but a very slippery key. At their next meeting, Westervelt was indignant because he had been dragged from his job to headquarters, and Walling was in a fury. The superintendent had ordered Westervelt's arrest because he'd learned the informer had known all along where Martha Mosher was living. Why had he witheld this important information? Westervelt blandly reminded Walling that he had agreed only to help capture Douglas, not his sister's husband.

Walling was stuck. He was party to the blood-is-thicker-than-water deal. If he was going to get any further help from Westervelt, he had to do it Westervelt's way. He cooled down and amity was restored. Westervelt gave evidence of his good intentions by coming up with a list of saloons where Mosher and Douglas hung out. And to prove his support of the treaty, Walling arranged a reinstatement interview with the police board for the informer.

In Philadelphia, the strategy committee continued to meet and ponder Walling's progress reports, but without Christian Ross. The unremitting strain of the passing months had proved too much for him. He had broken down physically and mentally, and was confined to his bed. Sarah Ross's brothers, Henry and Joseph Lewis, took over the family's end of the case. These strong-minded businessmen at first cooperated with the Philadelphia committee, then, as they became disgusted with the self-righteous attitude of their peers, struck out on their own.

On September 25, the kidnappers unexpectedly renewed their correspondence: "if yu compel us to put him to death yu shall receive a letter in 24 ours after where yu will find his body . . ."

The Lewises took this seriously and replied, accepting the kidnappers' terms. And they meant it. This did not sit well with the authorities, who had not deviated from their original attitude. But the Lewises were determined to do it their way. They were not impressed by the arguments that had overwhelmed Ross. Not even the optimistic reports from Walling could budge them.

The truth of the matter was that Walling's optimism rested on a shifty foundation. All he had to go on was Westervelt, but he didn't really have him. A bartender reported that the two suspects had made several recent visits to his saloon, during which they had huddled with Westervelt. When Walling confronted his ally with this evidence of complicity, the informer had a glib explanation. The meetings were accidental and so brief that he hadn't an opportunity to call the police. But he gave his word that if he ran into them again, he'd notify Walling immediately. What could Walling do?

The Lewis brothers received their final, detailed instructions from the kidnappers on October 31. The twenty thousand dollars in small bills was to be taken to New York. The bearer should advertise what hotel he was stopping at. He should remain there until their agent came for the money. Within hours after the ransom was paid, Charley would be released with a label on his back.

Though the Lewises were determined to go through with the transaction despite the committee's disapproval, they were not yet ready to break completely with the committee. They agreed reluctantly to try to bargain further with the kidnappers, who refused to budge from their position. It took almost three weeks before the Lewises declared their independence from the committee and went to New York with the ransom. Unfortunately, as it turned out, they compromised their freedom by informing the authorities of the coming transaction.

The Lewises, with a valise crammed with twenty thousand dollars in unmarked small bills, registered at the Fifth Avenue Hotel in New York on the night of November 17. They duly communicated their whereabouts to the kidnappers as ordered. They remained in their room all day and night of the eighteenth. No emissary came to collect the ransom.

Deeply disappointed and convinced that the authorities were right—you could not deal honestly with criminals—they checked out and took themselves back to Philadelphia. What they did not know was that Philadelphia had informed New York, and that Walling had had the hotel infiltrated by dozens of detectives. So much for honest dealing.

Once again in accord with the committee, the Lewis

family put an ad in the *New York Herald* on the nineteenth of November: "We have performed our part. You have broken faith. We will have no more trifling. Action must now be taken simultaneous."

Strong words, but shouted into a void. They waited for a reply. They knew on the basis of previous experience that an answer would be forthcoming. There was no immediate reply.

There was never to be a reply.

Walling was beside himself with anger. He accused Westervelt of having tipped off Mosher and Douglas about the police stakeout in the hotel. Westervelt denied it. Once again, Walling accepted his informer's protestations of innocence. Westervelt, crooked as he was, was still his best hope. The superintendent continued to believe that he was just a step behind the criminals, and that if he handled Westervelt properly he'd catch them.

Less than a month later society caught up with Mosher and Douglas on Long Island, when they tripped the burglar alarm in the Van Brunt summer home. The newspapers, the police, and the public agreed unanimously that double justice had been done. When the Van Brunts and their hired hands blasted the housebreakers, they had, though inadvertently, also punished the kidnappers of Charley Ross.

There was no one except Mosher's grief-stricken widow who doubted that Mosher had stolen Charley. Euphoric with relief that the case had been solved, the nation disregarded a fundamental tenet of American justice—that guilt must be proven beyond a reasonable doubt. Mosher and Douglas never had their day in court before a jury of their peers. No one was ever to hear their defense.

With the kidnappers out of the way, all that remained was to find Charley. At first the police reasoned that whoever was keeping the boy would hasten to let him go, in fear of the same fate that Mosher and his partner had met. Charley would be home by Christmas, they predicted. But that didn't happen. And the New Year came, but it was not a very happy occasion for the police because Charley was still missing, and the press and public had begun to turn against them.

It had begun to dawn on the man and woman in the street that the police achievement thus far was zero. All their efforts, schemes and stratagems to find the kidnappers had been useless. If it hadn't been for vigilant citizens, Mosher and Douglas would still have been alive. Unless Charley was found right quick police heads ought to roll.

Walling, who had been busy taking unjustified bows for the death of the suspects, felt the pressure most keenly. He came down as hard as he could on Westervelt who swore he had no knowledge about where the boy was. Walling had to come up with something to divert criticism from himself, and he came up with Westervelt. On the pretext that Christian Ross wanted to talk to him, Walling got Westervelt to go to Philadelphia. There were police waiting for him on his arrival. He was arrested and imprisoned, charged with abduction and conspiracy to abduct. Walling was to be the main witness against him.

Christian Ross got out of bed to visit Westervelt in jail.

When he came out, he told reporters that Westervelt had said, "Charley was alive when Mosher was killed." "As for myself," Ross added, "it would be a relief to know of his fate—whether dead or alive."

On August 30, 1875, Westervelt took his place in the dock and pleaded not guilty to all the charges. The prosecution, recognizing it had not the slightest circumstantial case of abduction, concentrated on Westervelt's complicity with Mosher and Douglas. The dangerous game Westervelt had played with Walling now became damning evidence against him when the superintendent testified. The principal issue in the case was the district attorney's contention that Westervelt had consistently misled the police and shielded the kidnappers in order to get a share of the ransom money. In opposition, the defense argued that Walling was using Westervelt as a scapegoat to cover up his ineptness. Westervelt was on the stand for four days, insisting that he had cooperated with the police.

The defense rested its case after a final question: "William Westervelt, can you now furnish, or could you at any time have furnished any clue to the abduction of the child, Charles Brewster Ross?"

"No. I wish to God I could," the defendant answered.

The jury were unable to agree on a verdict and the case was adjourned for a weekend. When they returned, the foreman announced they had found Westervelt innocent of abduction, but guilty of conspiracy to abduct, to extort money and to deprive Charley of his liberty.

On October 9, 1875, Judge Elcock gave Westervelt the maximum sentence allowed by law—seven years of solitary

confinement at hard labor. Ross dragged himself down to the prison and promised to help Westervelt get a pardon, if he had any information about Charley, alive or dead. Westervelt swore that he knew nothing.

In January 1881 model prisoner William Westervelt, with a year off for good behavior, was released from prison. He still maintained his innocence, and pledged he would devote himself to finding Charley. But nothing further was ever heard from him.

The hunt for Charley Ross went on during the following decades. More supposed Charleys kept turning up, and Christian Ross continued to check them out, unwilling to leave any possibility uninvestigated. His quest for his son ended only with his death in 1897.

Sarah Ross continued the search into the twentieth century when her little boy would have grown into a middle-aged man. As she grew too feeble to travel, she sent her brothers to talk to forty-year-olds who said they were Charley.

In 1943, Charley's big brother Walter, a retired stockbroker, reported that the parade of claimants was still continuing. Over the years more than five thousand boys and men had identified themselves as Charley Ross. A century after the four-year-old was stolen, an item occasionally appears in the press about someone who says he is a great-grandson of Charley Ross. But the question of what happened to the real Charley Ross remains unanswered.

One of the recent claimants to the identity of Charley Ross, a man known as Gustave Blair.

THE VANISHING BONES:
The Double Disappearance of Peking Man

•

ALTHOUGH IT IS no longer the world's tallest man-made structure, the Empire State Building, which rises a quarter of a mile above Fifth Avenue and Thirty-fourth Street in New York City, continues to attract millions of visitors to the observatory on the one hundred second floor. The view on a clear day is spectacular. You can see fifty miles in every direction except south, where the twin peaks of the Trade Center loom up in the way at the tip of Manhattan.

Since it was topped out in 1931 the skyscraper has been the site of a lot of action. It has, for example, been struck by airplanes, human flies have tried to walk up its sides, kids have tried to spit down from its dizzying heights, and so on. And of course it has been used as a trysting place by innumerable romantically inclined couples.

By far the most famous pair ever to occupy the tower

top were a lovesick monster gorilla, ten basketball centers high, King Kong—from the movie of the same name—and the beautiful woman-sized object of his unrequited affection, played by Fay Wray. The world will long remember the tragic end of that star-crossed romance: Kong nobly protecting Fay while being shot down from the summit by an armada of United States Air Force fighters. But most, if not all, visiting couples are likely to be better assorted, somewhat less noticeable.

Into this stuffy category you would have put the dowdy housewife type and the prosperous businessman type who had their heads together in a corner of the observatory on the afternoon of June 27, 1973. That's supposing you noticed them at all.

There was no obvious reason to look again, except that they were more mature than most courting couples—she in her forties, he some twenty years older. But they didn't behave like most couples, either. The lady kept a wary eye on anyone who came near, then suddenly, terrified, bolted for the elevator. Her companion, caught flatfooted, gave chase, but in vain.

Well, there's nothing so extraordinary about a couple quarreling and breaking up, temporarily or permanently. It happens often in real life. And in movie life it is standard operating procedure. But as it happens, this particular scene would not have worked in a movie, because it led to no happy ending—nor to any ending at all.

Besides, it would be terribly difficult for a filmmaker to create a believable script if he stuck to the facts: A tycoon turned private eye at sixty to find persons missing a half-million years before he was born; involved in his quest were relics simultaneously worthless and beyond price. Three great powers were at loggerheads. The United States Marines came to the rescue and had to be rescued. Dead men, women and children told tales. Scholars staked reputations on dragon bones.

The characters are real enough. Take the man on the top of the Empire State. His name was and is Christopher G. Janus, Chicago stockbroker, self-made millionaire, philanthropist—the money behind a foundation devoted to international exchange. There was nothing mysterious about him until he took it upon himself to solve the mystery.

Mr. Janus was on a cultural exchange mission to the People's Republic of China in the spring of 1973 when, as he was to report, a high government official took him away from a reception and said: "Help us find Peking Man. If you can return Peking Man to us, you will be a hero to the Chinese people."

If he became a hero to 800 million Chinese, Mr. Janus reasoned, it would doubtless help better relations between China and the U.S.A. So Mr. Janus blithely said he would be glad to oblige. Since he had never heard of the missing man, he hadn't the remotest notion of what he was getting himself into.

Mr. Janus soon learned that his mission was not the kind of thing a police missing persons bureau could help him with. Just for starters, Peking Man had vanished twice— the first time in 500,000 B.C.; the second, after he had reappeared and been around for fifteen years, in 1941. Another unique aspect of his disappearance both times is that his entire family—some forty persons of both sexes and various ages—went with him.

Some of Mr. Janus's information came from scholarly journals, some from the press. His most authoritative source was the amateur detective who had headed up the investigation for more than thirty years, Dr. Harry L. Shapiro. An eminent scientist, chairman of the Department of Anthropology at the American Museum of Natural History, Dr. Shapiro had not abandoned hope that Peking Man could and would be located.

Shapiro's optimism was not based on the emergence of any new, promising leads. If he refused to be dismayed, it must have been because, impossible as the solution to the '41 disappearance seemed, it was a snap compared to the earlier one. This time they knew they were looking for Peking Man. The investigators in the 1920s didn't know he was missing. In fact, they didn't even know that he had ever existed.

How can you possibly find someone whose existence is unknown? Well, first you have to believe in dragon bones. *Dragon* bones? Sure, just hop down to the drugstore. In pre-revolutionary China they were sold for a few yen, without a doctor's prescription. Ground to a powder, and taken as directed by your neighborhood pharmacist, they were supposed to cure anything and everything that ailed you.

The trail that led to the discovery of Peking Man began in the late 1920s in Chou Kou Tien drugstore, some thirty miles from Peking. The scientists who were browsing along the dragon bone counter stumbled upon a couple of bones that seemed different from the everyday assortment. All the others were the petrified remains of prehistoric creatures. This pair of fossils stunned the browsers. They resembled, or seemed to resemble, human teeth.

The scientists were no more prepared for this than Columbus was to find the New World sticking up out of the ocean. Science had never considered the possibility that a branch of the human family tree had sprouted in China. Concealing their excitement, so as not to raise the price, the scientists bought the molars for intensive laboratory study.

Meanwhile, the wholesaler who supplied bones to the drugstore was tracked down, and he led to his source of supply—a mound known to the local residents as Chicken Bone Hill. The surrounding area was a mine of fossilized remains of saber-toothed tigers and other extinct animals. Interesting specimens but disappointing. It took a lot of digging back through time before the scientists found what they were looking for—proof that creatures like humans had lived out their lives in this part of the world ages ago.

There wasn't much to go on at first, three molars in all. Hardly enough for a distinguished scientist to risk his career and reputation on. Nevertheless, Dr. Davidson Black, head of Peking Union Medical College, under whose auspices the dig was being conducted, stuck his neck out and gained scientific immortality. He could just as easily have achieved oblivion for the uncompromisingly blunt, revolutionary announcement he made in 1927: "The actual presence of early man in Eastern Asia is no longer a matter of conjecture."

Strong words for a scientist, especially for one who had

Excavations at Chou Kou Tien. Skull fragments of Peking Man were discovered in the roped-off area at right.

no formal training in the required special fields of archaeology, paleontology, geology. Black had an M.D. from a Canadian university. His reputation was based upon his unquestionable contributions as an anatomist. The kindest thing the specialists could find to say about him after his dramatic pronouncement was that as an amateur he didn't know what he was doing, and that like so many well-meaning novices he had an obsession about the origin of the human species.

It was certainly true that Black was a man with a twelve-year-old obsession. In 1914, he had made a trip to England to study with the preeminent anatomist Professor Elliot Smith. Black became fascinated by a project Smith was working on—restoring the head of a prehistoric man out of fossil fragments that had been unearthed in Piltdown, England, three years earlier.

Working on Piltdown Man affected young Dr. Black the way a concert or a tennis match can influence many young people. But most of us give up our dreams of becoming Van Cliburn or Billie Jean King. Black never gave up his dream of finding the missing link in the human chain.

If Black had known the truth about Piltdown Man, whose discovery had revolutionized science, he would not have been so inspired, and Peking Man would never have been discovered. At the very least our common ancestor's reentrance would have been postponed indefinitely. For Piltdown Man was a phony. The supposedly ancient skull fragments were those of a modern man, aged as some "antiques" are given extra years by unscrupulous antique dealers. And the bits of his jaw were those of an ape.

Black's illusion was never to be dissipated. He died in 1934, and the fraud was discovered by a pair of British scientists, who had kept restudying the bone pieces, in 1955. But Piltdown Man remained enthroned in science during Black's lifetime. Ironically, Black's establishment critics kept pointing out that a few teeth were hardly conclusive proof of the existence of Peking Man—especially in comparison to the much more significant skull and jawbones of Piltdown Man.

It wasn't until 1929 that Peking Man came close to matching Piltdown's eminence. It was fitting that crowning evidence of Peking Man's existence, a sizeable hunk of his skull, was found by a Chinese member of Black's staff—Dr. W. C. Pei. Vindication, but not enough for Black and his colleagues. They continued to scrape and sift back through

A composite plaster skull of Peking Man, composed of castings of fragments from both male and female individuals.

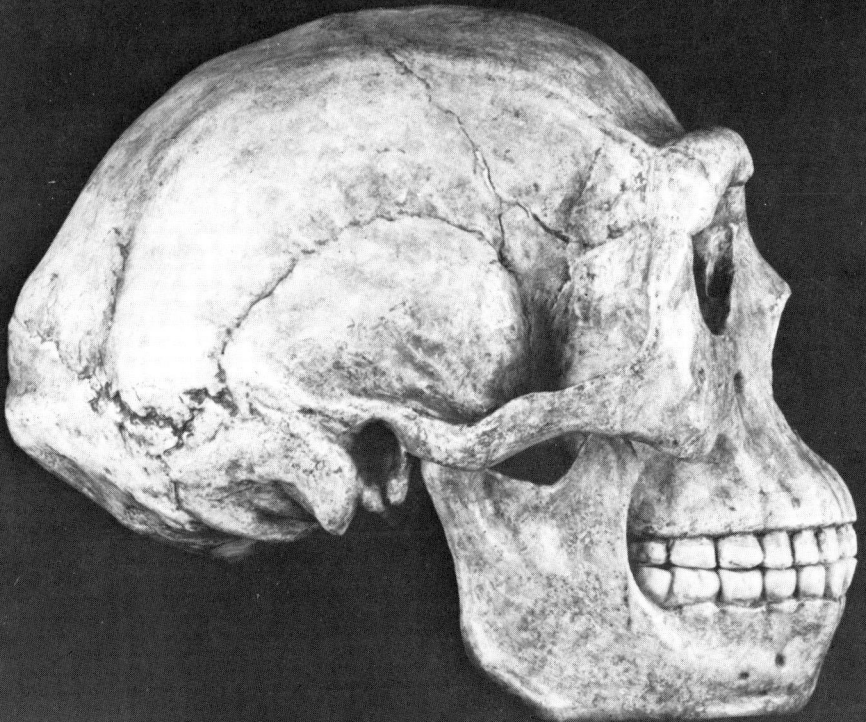

geologic time, stopping only occasionally when they were caught in the line of fire between battling Chinese war-lords.

By the time the Japanese occupation of China in 1937 had put a permanent halt to the excavation, Black's expedition had bit by bit accumulated a priceless scientific trea-sure—by far the largest collection of proofs of the existence of a vanished branch of the human family tree. Previous to this time, the theory of the evolutionary descent or ascent of man depended upon the scanty fragmented remains of single individuals. These bones had been left by a whole tribe, forty creatures enough akin to us to know the uses of fire.

Davidson Black's abundant proof that *Sinanthropus pe-kinensis* ("Chinese man from Peking") was a distant relative of modern *Homo sapiens* ("Wise man") made a big impres-sion on the scientific community, but none at all on those who took the Bible literally. The fundamentalists believed that the Almighty had, as it says in the gospel, created man out of dust, and woman out of his rib. They had not been budged by the skull chips of *Homo neanderthalensis* ("Neanderthal man") found in Germany in 1857, nor by those of *Pithecanthropus erectus* ("Ape-man who stands erect") dug out of the Javanese earth in 1891.

The scientists who manned Peking Medical College's Cenozoic Research Laboratory labeled, photographed and made casts of every precious bit of their treasure. No mor-tal remains were ever so honored, so artfully tended, so watched over. Yet despite all the attention given him, de-spite the fact that his guardians knew that he was in danger and had done everything to protect him, Peking Man had disappeared.

By the time Mr. Janus took it upon himself to find him, over thirty years later, Peking Man had long been out of the eye of the press, and everybody had given him up, with the single exception of Dr. Shapiro. The scientist recognized that the stockbroker's optimism more than matched his own, though it came from a different life-style. Janus's confidence that the mystery could be solved was based upon his conviction that money—which he was amply supplied with—could work miracles; and it was precisely a miracle that was required in this case.

It's an understatement to say the circumstances were mind-boggling. The remnants of Peking Man had last been seen when they were packed away in two boxes by their laboratory custodians in late November, 1941. Again and again during the preceding year as war threatened, the scientists had tried to have the bones removed to the United States for safekeeping, and this was their last desperate attempt to remove the treasure from jeopardy by getting it out of the country.

There were great difficulties in the way. All the research was funded by the Rockefeller Foundation and based on agreement with the Chinese government that the fossils were to remain in their native land. Consequently, any move to take the precious bones out of China would be a violation of the agreement, and would subject them to confiscation by customs. Under the chaotic wartime conditions that existed, the scholars didn't dare risk letting Peking Man fall into bureaucratic hands.

One way to protect the find from molestation was to have it sent out in a diplomatic pouch. Urgent pleas for such a safe conduct were made to the American ambassador, Nelson Johnson, but he understandably had other priorities.

There was one final way out for the fossils. A detachment of United States Marines were preparing to ship out for the Philippines, and it was arranged the boxes would go with them. The boxes were sent care of Pharmacist's Mate Herman Davis at Camp Holcomb, in Chingwangtao. Davis and his buddies were already packed to leave, and he put the two boxes, which were almost identical with Marine footlockers, along with his own stuff where he could keep a watchful eye on them.

Neither Davis nor the seventeen others in the medical unit nor the fossil footlockers ever reached the Philippines. It wouldn't have mattered much if they had, because the next day Japanese war planes bombed Pearl Harbor, and not long after the Philippines were captured. Davis and his group found themselves prisoners of war in a Tientsin camp.

It took a while before the Japanese got around to sending the prisoners their belongings from Camp Holcomb. And when Davis got his, he discovered his personal baggage had been looted, and the two footlockers he had guarded had not arrived. There was nothing he could do about it.

Was Peking Man a casualty of World War II? Had the enemy soldiers who'd scavenged through the Marines' possessions thrown the old bones away? They stole only what was valuable, or useful. You couldn't expect a Japanese infantryman to know the scientific value of the contents of the boxes, could you? Well, no—and yes.

Even before the outbreak of hostilities between the United States and Japan, Japanese scientists had shown an acquisitive interest in Peking Man, proud evidence that our species was born in Asia. They were able through the Japanese military presence in China to keep a close watch on the work going on at Peking Medical College, but couldn't interfere with it because correct diplomatic relations had to be maintained with the United States. However, after Pearl Harbor, no holds were barred. The Japanese Imperial High Command gave the bones top priority as a prize of war. It seems improbable that the disciplined Japanese troops would discard the fossils the officers were searching for. And if the bones had been found at Camp Holcomb or along the route to the prison, they might well have been sent to Tokyo.

All the questions about the vanished bones had to remain unanswered during the next four years of bloody warfare. Three months after the original, primitive atom bombs turned Hiroshima and Nagasaki back to the Stone Age, the *New York Times* came up with a solution to the mystery. SAVE PEKING MAN RELICS, read a November 20, 1945, headline. The story filed by the *Times* man in Tokyo reported that the fossils had been found among other war loot at Tokyo Imperial University. Two weeks later the discovery was confirmed by *Newsweek* magazine's correspondent in Shanghai: PEKING MAN IS SAFE.

There was jubilation in the halls of the Museum of Natural History. And indeed fossils from the dig at Chou Kou

Tien which had been taken by the Japanese from the college laboratory were found in Tokyo. But they were the remains of the animals Peking Man had hunted, and the stone tools he had used. Of the body he had inhabited, there was no trace.

The postwar search in Japan, occupied by the American military, got nowhere. The logical place to look was China, and approaches were made to the United States State Department for assistance. But the State Department was not responsive. Even if the diplomats had been, the civil war that broke out in China after the Japanese had surrendered effectively prevented any investigation.

Through the years, Dr. Shapiro and his colleagues kept following up every lead, no matter how slight. One story that astounded them was that Peking Man had been stolen by Americans and was in the possession of Dr. Shapiro. To this charge, made by the People's Republic of China, Dr. Shapiro gave the press a one-word refutation: "Nonsense."

What the Museum of Natural History had was the sole remaining evidence that Peking Man had existed—casts, photographs, measurements of his skull and skeleton which had been removed from the laboratories and taken to the United States shortly before the outbreak of war with Japan.

The American scientists would have liked to pick up the trail of the missing bones on the site where they had been lost. But during the period of the cold war with Mao Tse-tung's China, they hadn't any chance of being admitted to that land. With detente, there was some hope. The first indication that China was interested in a cooperative hunt with the Americans was the Chinese overture to Mr. Janus.

The approach Janus proposed to Dr. Shapiro at their meeting was something no previous investigators had tried, or even thought of: Buy a solution to the case; offer a reward. A man of action, he no sooner said it than it was done. The press carried the announcement: Five thousand dollars for the return, or information leading to the return, of Peking Man or any part of him.

Money produced a lot of talk, mostly from people who didn't know what they were talking about but who were attracted by an easy five thousand dollars. But there was one phone call, from a woman who wouldn't give her name, that rang some bells.

"I'm the widow of a Marine officer," she whispered. "When he died, he left me a footlocker with some skull and bone fragments he had gotten in China."

No other response to the reward offer had come so close to the facts of the case. Janus tried unsuccessfully to get more details. He invited the caller to lunch. Refused. Her voice was thin with fear. Of what, Janus could not make out. He proposed several other meeting places, at her convenience. She turned them all down. They were getting nowhere, until she suggested the top of the Empire State Building. How would he know her? He wouldn't. She'd know him.

Janus could not be at all sure that his blind date would show up. So he was more than pleasantly surprised when, some minutes after he got off the last elevator stop, an attractive woman in her forties gestured to him.

Janus followed her through the crowd of camera-wielding

tourists into a corner of the observatory. He assured her that he had come alone, and she plunged hurriedly into her story.

Her husband had confessed to her, before he died, that the footlocker contained loot—valuable loot he had stolen from China—and warned her that she could get into serious trouble for possessing it. After his death, she'd opened the box and saw only the bones. She couldn't figure out what he had been talking about, and had kept the bones only as a memento of the departed. It wasn't until she read about the reward that she realized how valuable her legacy was.

In proof, she dug into her pocketbook and produced a photograph of the top layer of the contents of an old footlocker. Janus could recognize some skull and bone fragments, but had no idea whether they were those he was looking for. To his unscientific eye they looked human and fossilized, and his excitement grew. Where were they? When could they be seen? Before he made a deal, she must realize he had to have more than a photograph.

Fair enough? Yes. But before she answered any of his questions, he must agree to raise the reward offer. Accustomed as he was to negotiating matters involving six, seven and more figures, Janus was nevertheless appalled to hear her evaluation of the fossils' worth—$500 million. Of course, that could only be the asking price. He had just begun to bargain with her when a flashbulb popped somewhere near them, and the woman snatched the photo of the bones from him and vanished.

When Janus reported the abortive meeting to Dr. Sha-

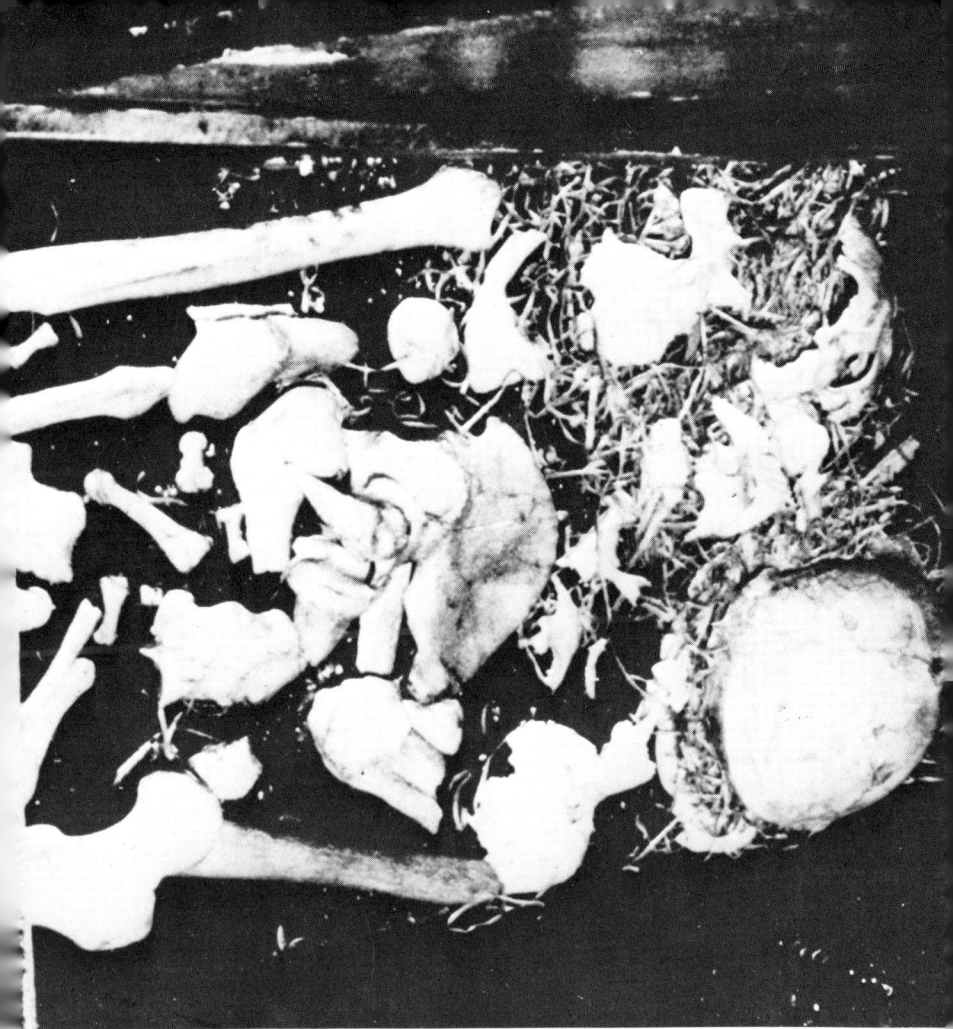

This photograph was offered by the mystery woman as proof that the missing bones were in her possession.

piro, both agreed that the photograph might have been a fake. Nevertheless, they agreed that the negotiations should be resumed if possible. If Janus heard from the woman again, he should insist, tactfully of course, that before any money pass hands, the bones be examined by Dr. Shapiro or some other scientist qualified to authenticate them.

Since Janus had no idea where the anonymous woman could be reached, all he could do was wait for her to surface. After a month had passed, time enough for her to have realized he hadn't been trying to trap her on the tower, Janus tried to renew their brief acquaintance. His cryptic ad appeared where it was hard to miss, at the bottom of the first page of the *New York Times*, August 4, 1972: "PEKING MAN Emp. $1? Obs. mtg. Funds avail; no questions. Phone C. G. J.—Advt."

"I didn't really have much hope," Janus was to tell a *Times* reporter, "but sure enough it must have been a week later when I got a call from the woman.

"I asked her to send me a copy of the picture so I could have the fossils authenticated. She was reluctant. She said, 'How do I know someone will not authenticate them away from me?'

"Several times she spoke of the fossils being stolen property. Those were her words: 'stolen property.' "

Janus must have been very persuasive, because the mystery woman sent him a copy of the photograph that had excited him. With it in hand he hurried to Dr. Shapiro's office.

All that Dr. Shapiro would commit himself to was: "I

have a strong suspicion that it's interesting. The skull has the shape of the Peking Man."

Dr. Shapiro's careful non-commitment was to be expected in the modus operandi of scientist-detectives. But another respected member of the scientific community was less circumspect. Professor William Howells, a leading paleontologist, scrutinized the photograph and reported the skull, in his opinion, was definitely of the genus *Sinanthropus pekinensis*. He went further to positively identify it as Skull Fragment #XI.

What Janus had to contend with now was the widow's fear that she would wind up in jail for trying to dispose of stolen property. He took care of this by getting a widely publicized statement from the United States State Department. An assistant secretary for educational and cultural affairs pointed out to the widow through the press that "the statute of limitations has expired," and thus, "the Federal Government would not be interested in prosecution."

He also appealed to the missing woman's patriotism: "I hope you will be able to persuade the lady in question that she will be doing not only her duty but a genuine service to the United States, in coming forward with the fossils to make them available for return to the People's Republic of China."

That should have done it, but it didn't. There was no response. Only temporarily disappointed, Mr. Janus energetically followed up other leads. One came from a Chinese businessman in New York who informed Janus, "A friend of mine, a high official in the Chinese Nationalist Government in Taiwan, has the footlocker containing the bones."

The informant, who insisted on anonymity, quoted his official chum: "He said there was a great deal of violence connected with getting these fossils and the family is terribly afraid." Janus was able to gather that the fear of violence could be assuaged for the right price.

Well, this was a somewhat promising lead. It was known that when the Nationalist Chinese fled from the Communists, they naturally took with them anything of value they could carry. Why not Peking Man?

Janus took off for Taiwan. His aide in the Taiwanese press raised the ante for the return of the bones to $150,000.00. There was not even a crackpot response. This did not necessarily mean that the informant had been misinformed. But no one in that police state would have dared to admit he had the fossils and was willing to return them to the American who had promised them to the enemy Communist Chinese.

Janus hoped to overcome this problem by announcing to the Taiwanese reporters, "I certainly don't want the bones to go to the Communists." This could not have helped him achieve his original intention of improving relations with the People's Republic. From the diplomatic point of view, it was perhaps just as well that Peking Man didn't turn up in Taiwan.

As time passed, and the widow did not reappear, Janus decided to run the risk of her disapproval by enlisting the

Christopher Janus, still in pursuit of the bones, poses with a plaster cast of Peking Man's skull.

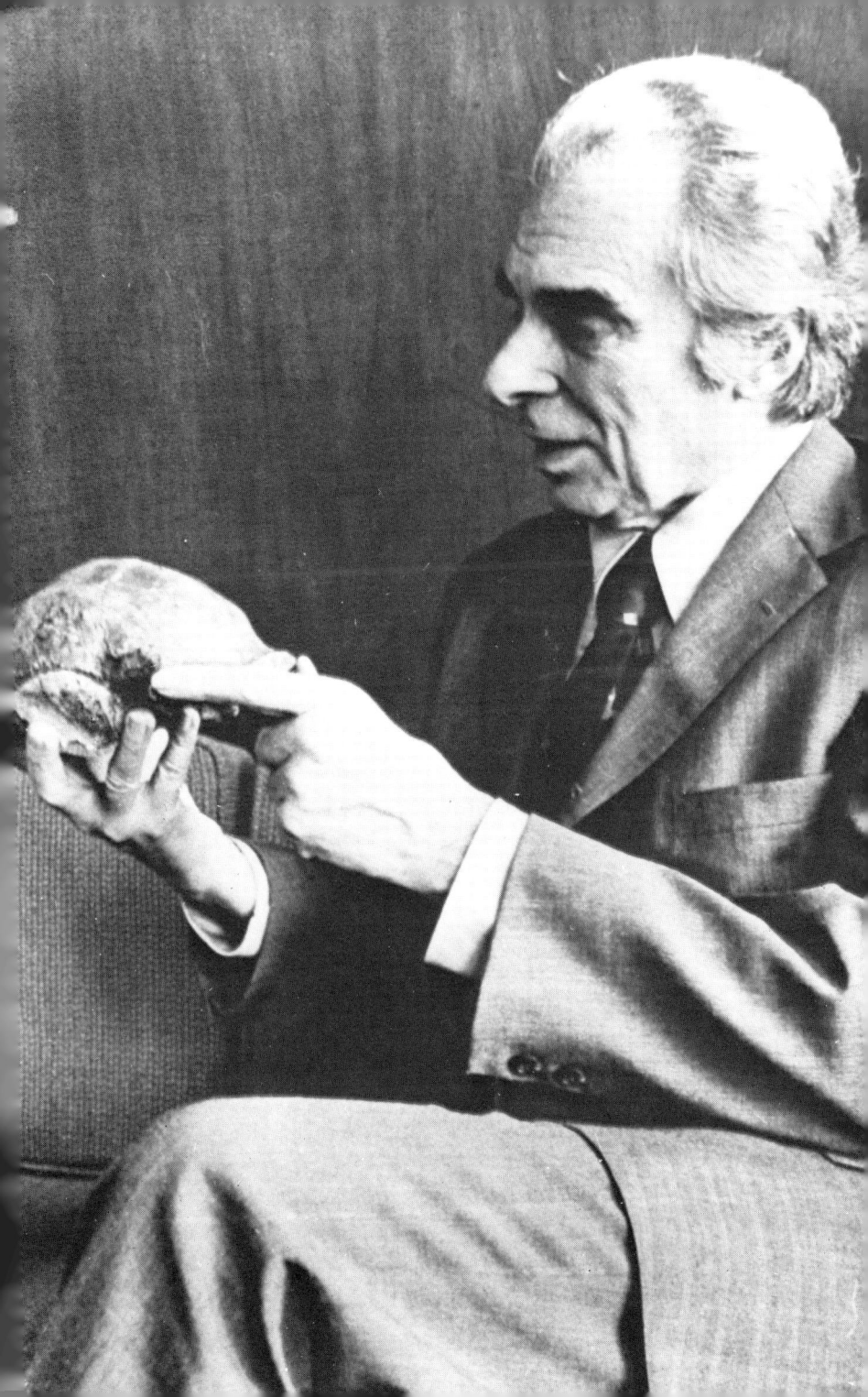

FBI to explore the Marine connection. The special agents could find no clues to her from Marine sources. Janus flew out to a reunion of the Camp Holcomb Marine detachment in Dayton, Ohio. The veterans were a mine of information about the bad old days of their surrender to the Japanese, but they were no help to Janus. One former leatherneck who was most knowledgeable about the Chinese customs guessed, "Peking Man was long ago dispensed to an ailing Chinese in the form of medicine."

If the fossils had been found by a lay prospector for dragon bones in the debris of war, and sold to a drugstore, the trail had come full circle. Some folks who are mystically inclined believe Peking Man resented being disturbed from his grave, and therefore welcomed being turned into medicine, to be swallowed and so vanish forever.

But Dr. Shapiro seems not to accept this solution. That would be giving up. He's not ready to do that. For all anyone knows the boxes may have been hidden in some unlikely place in China and will some day be found.

And Janus still has not given up on the vanished woman, though several years have passed since he saw her. Time has tempered his original enthusiasm. He's willing to say: "This whole thing may be a hoax, but again, I believe she may just have Peking Man."

THE MA & PA MURDERS:
The Lizzie Borden Case

•

FOR MANY YEARS after the double murder in Fall River, Massachusetts, little girls all over the country jumped rope to the cheerful rhythm of an anonymous ditty. In four lines it gives the generally accepted solution to the horrendous crime committed on August 4, 1892:

> "Lizzie Borden took an axe
> And gave her mother forty whacks,
> And when she saw what she had done
> She gave her father forty-one."

Like many present-day singing commercials, the catchy jingle can't stand very close examination. Some of the details are inaccurate. For one thing, the slain woman, Abby Borden, was not Lizzie's mother but her stepmother. For another, the number of blows is greatly exaggerated. A panel of Harvard experts counted fewer than a dozen. And finally—and most important—Lizzie was tried by the Commonwealth of Massachusetts, and was found innocent.

In the case of an unsolved murder police usually keep all the relevant material in an open file, and the search for the murderer continues. But so far as anyone knows, the police made no further attempt to solve the crime after Lizzie was acquitted. Nor was anyone else ever tried. Of course it isn't unusual for a prosecutor to give up on a case when he has failed to prove his prime suspect guilty. His chances for convincing a jury that he is right the second time, when he was wrong the first, are negligible.

What makes the Fall River murders different from any other unsolved crimes is that not long after Lizzie Borden walked out of the courthouse a free woman, self-appointed professional and amateur investigators began trying to reverse the verdict. And they're still trying. Lawyers, playwrights, poets, novelists have not been able to let the dead rest. The artistic insistence on Lizzie's guilt has extended even into the ballet, created by choreographer Agnes De Mille a half century after Lizzie's exoneration. The now classic dance drama called *Fall River Legend* begins and ends with a gallows scene, and the dancer who portrays Lizzie wears a costume splattered with blood. Lizzie Borden has become a horrifying American folk figure—a monster who committed the unforgivable crime: murdering her parents.

Unlike the Fall River police, who arrested Lizzie because she was the most obvious suspect, many contemporary investigators find her guilty by analyzing her unconscious mind. Probings of this sort, even by psychiatrists, are necessarily speculative, and however ingenious hardly constitute evidence.

Perhaps she must be found guilty, for what the case comes down to is if Lizzie didn't kill Abby and Andrew Borden, who did? Well, there was her uncle John Morse, whom Fall River suspected so strongly at first that he was almost lynched. And Bridget Sullivan, the Borden housemaid. And there was that young stranger who was seen hanging around the Borden house that bloody day. He was never found, never identified. And what about the numerous enemies Andrew Borden had made on his way from rags to riches?

It was not difficult to dislike and even hate Andrew Borden. Though the well-to-do residents of Fall River regarded him as an uplifting example of what Yankee thrift and shrewdness could accomplish, they had contempt for his miserliness. The son of a fish peddler, he had started out in life as an embalmer, and though he rose to become a bank president, mill owner and slum landlord, the graveside manner of his beginning remained with him. Tall, gaunt, always dressed in black, he was a caricature of an undertaker.

At the time of his sudden death Borden had accumulated half a million dollars by his ruthless though legal methods of doing business. Among his legion of ill-wishers were the small businessmen he had ruined, the mill hands he had relentlessly exploited, the tenants he had evicted and the debtors from whom he had exacted usurious interest.

Andrew J. Borden.

There were many in Fall River who were not saddened by his death, and more who regretted that it had not come sooner.

If there were many who might have had reason to hasten Andrew Borden's departure from life, quite the reverse was true about the other victim. The citizens of Fall River knew she was Andrew's wife and the stepmother of his two daughters, but they only really became aware of her existence when she was killed. She rarely left her house, had no friends, no interests, no life of her own. The only activity she engaged in, apart from keeping house, was overeating. Today's weight watchers might say that Abby ate so much because she was deprived of any other emotional satisfaction. Whatever the cause, she was grotesque—barely five feet tall, she weighed well over two hundred pounds. She was so ponderous that she would not have been agile enough to avoid the attacker's axe, even if she'd had the opportunity.

Nobody seems to have had much feeling about Abby, one way or another, except Lizzie. Witnesses at the trial testified that Lizzie had come to hate her. They agreed, however, that the relationship between the two had been harmonious, up until almost the end.

Abby was the only mother Lizzie ever knew, her own having died when she was born. Lizzie was two, and her sister Emma twelve, when Andrew made Abby his wife. By the standards of the time, Fall River agreed Abby was lucky. It was probably the only offer the plain thirty-eight-year-old spinster had ever had. Also by standards of the time, Andrew Borden had made a sensible deal. Abby

Abby D. Borden.

cooked his meals, kept his house and took care of his children. She was careful with his money, never questioned his decisions, knew her place and never budged from it. Not once in thirty years did she give him cause to complain. And there's no reason to doubt she would have gone right on being a model wife if she had been allowed to live to a riper age.

Abby's vegetable existence seems to have influenced the older girl more than it did the younger. Emma may have patterned herself on Abby because, being ten years older than Lizzie, she mothered her little sister. In any event, when her parents were struck down, Emma was forty-two, evidently not likely to marry. She had few friends and went out almost as infrequently as her stepmother.

Lizzie was different from the other occupants of the somber Borden house on Second Street. Though her ungainly figure and heavy features did not attract gentlemen callers—at thirty-two she was still single—she did not let that inhibit her. She dressed well and had a busy social life. She had many friends who knew her as a warm, kind, and loving person. When there was church welfare work to be done, Lizzie could be counted on to volunteer. It was not only among those of her own station that Lizzie was admired and respected. She was also well thought of on the wrong side of the tracks because of her efforts on behalf of the poor and unfortunate. It was no wonder, then, that Fall River was appalled when Lizzie was arrested.

Was Lizzie a Jekyll-Hyde? Behind her open, friendly, selfless exterior was there a secret ogre? It's curious that those whose study of the murders has led them to condemn her affirm that she was exactly what she seemed. That is, until five years before she supposedly took axe in hand.

What happened back then in 1887 was that Andrew Borden made a real estate deal. Before consummating it, he talked the matter over with his first wife's brother John Morse, whom he trusted for the same virtues he found in himself. Morse was as miserly and rapacious as he. Andrew bought a house, and for reasons of his own, he put the house in Abby's name. He kept the matter a secret.

Though Andrew Borden was not renowned for dealing openly, and nobody knows how many such undercover transactions he'd made during his career, it is alleged that he kept this one secret because he thought his daughters would resent his favoring Abby over them. It's difficult to believe that he intended Abby to be anything but the nominal owner of the property. Nobody knew better than the sisters that Abby was their father's creature. How then could they have felt that Abby was depriving them of their inheritance?

Nevertheless, testimony tells us that both women were furious when the secret came out. Emma swallowed her anger. Lizzie, always the more forthright of the two, blamed Abby for having tricked Andrew into it. Nor did she hide her anger against her Uncle John, for having conspired against her and Emma. From then on the tepid temperature of the Borden menage turned icy. Lizzie stopped calling Abby "mother," and when she mentioned her at all, referred to her stiffly as Mrs. Borden.

This hostile atmosphere was maintained for four years.

Then the Borden house was robbed. Abby's watch and chain, her few pieces of jewelry, and about a hundred dollars Andrew kept locked in his desk were taken. Borden reported the crime to the police, but insisted it not be made public. In fact it was not known in Fall River until Lizzie talked about it to a friend, the day before the killings.

The robbery took place on one of the rare occasions when the parents were away. It resembles the "locked room" mysteries of fiction in which no one can presumably get in or out. Andrew had locked the doors, as he always did when he went out, closing in his daughters and Bridget. None of the women seem to have heard anything. Anti-Lizzie researchers conjecture that Lizzie turned thief to pay Abby and Andrew back—that he knew she'd done it and therefore called off the police.

Immediately preceding the murder there were two events which seem to implicate Lizzie further. Her father made another real estate deal, and Abby complained that she was being poisoned.

Just why Andrew should have been looking for additional troubles with his daughters, it's hard to comprehend. But once again he decided to put a piece of property into Abby's name, and let no one in on the secret except John Morse. Once again, Lizzie supposedly found out about it, and this time she supposedly plotted murder to prevent it.

A pharmacist was to testify that two weeks before the murders, Lizzie tried unsuccessfully to buy prussic acid from him. And the record shows that August 3, the day before the murders, Abby went to the doctor to complain she was being poisoned. On the other hand, it also shows that everybody in the household who had eaten the same dinner at noon got sick, including Lizzie. And that Abby's Dr. Bowen didn't take Abby's poisoning complaint seriously. Fall River was suffering a heat wave, and he diagnosed the cause of her problem as spoiled food.

Surprisingly, Lizzie seems to have disagreed with the doctor. She visited a friend the afternoon of August 3 and told her she thought someone was trying to poison the family. She chattered on about how the Borden barn had been broken into twice, and about the many enemies her father had made. It was on this occasion that Lizzie revealed for the first time the robbery of the year before. Was this outpouring of revelations part of the murder plan, a clumsy attempt to divert suspicion from herself?

The blistering heat of August 3 continued through the night and into the morning of August 4. Except for the weather, everything was as usual in the Borden household. Andrew Borden went downtown sometime after nine o'clock, and Abby was dusting the dining room when Lizzie appeared. They exchanged polite good mornings. Lizzie was still sick to her stomach and the maid Bridget even sicker. Abby instructed Bridget to wash the windows from the outside, and she went to work. Emma had not returned from an overnight visit. Thus, at the beginning of the day, Abby and Lizzie were alone inside the house.

Neighbors observed a young man loitering around the Borden house. While he was not under constant watch, the reports agreed he remained over a period of hours—the time, as it turned out, when the murders were committed. Those who dismiss the loiterer as a suspect point out that the murders were done a couple of hours apart. They say it is incredible that he would have entered the house, killed Abby, gone out, waited for Andrew to return and then cut him down. And it is incredible. But for that matter, how credible is it that a young woman of impeccable character and sound mind could have suddenly gone berserk and killed her parents? Yes, there are cases of presumably normal people going crazy, but they inevitably admit their guilt and plead insanity. Not Lizzie. Her insistence on her innocence and her sanity never wavered.

There is some evidence to prove that Andrew Borden waited downtown for his wife to put her signature on the deed. But when he returned home, and Bridget let him in, he didn't ask for his wife. Bridget assumed she was tidying up her bedroom. But Bridget was wrong. For almost two hours, Abby had been lying in her blood in the upstairs guest room.

From Bridget's testimony, we learn that Miss Lizzie came down dressed to go out. She was wearing her hat, and—what later seemed suspicious to the police—a heavy woolen dress, a garment hardly fit for the 110-degree day. Lizzie greeted her father, who went upstairs briefly, then joined her in the sitting room, where he stretched out on a sofa. Apparently Lizzie changed her mind about going out, for the last Bridget saw of them on her way up to the attic, Lizzie had taken off her hat and was ironing while Andrew was resting. If we believe Lizzie's account of what hap-

Abby Borden's body was discovered on the floor of the guest room.

pened in that room, darkened against the burning sun, she was the next-to-last person to see Andrew alive. If we don't, she was the last.

What is particularly fascinating about this case is that opposite conclusions are built upon the same foundation—the relationship that existed between father and daughter.

It is universally accepted that if Andrew Borden was capable of any act of love or generosity in his seventy years it never came to light. With one exception. He had a soft spot in his heart for the baby of the family. His feeling for her was so strong that it overcame his miserliness. Andrew denied her nothing. Lizzie could waste money on fripperies like dresses, shoes, hats. His extraordinary open-handedness went so far as to allow even such a spendthrift excess as a trip to Europe. For Andrew Borden—to whom, if money wasn't everything, it was the only thing—no greater proof of love was possible.

And there is no question that Lizzie loved her dour, taciturn father. This may even have had something to do with her not getting married, since in practical, hard-headed Fall River, far less attractive heiresses than Lizzie became brides. But Andrew seems to have been the only man in her life.

One concrete sign of the affection between father and daughter was the little gold class ring the girls at Fall River High School got when they graduated. Usually a girl gave the treasured memento to a boy she favored. Lizzie gave hers to her father. And Andrew, who had the undertaker's professional avoidance of ornament, never took Lizzie's ring off his little finger, indeed took it with him into his grave.

You'd think logically that Lizzie's love for her father would make it impossible for anyone to believe she'd harm him. But it is precisely because she loved him so dearly that some psychoanalytical speculations go against her. They take off from the discoveries made by Dr. Sigmund Freud, originator of psychoanalysis, who first explored the workings of the unconscious. Freud pointed out that it was normal for children to love their parents and sometimes to get angry with them and hate them. Moreover, it was characteristic of child-parent relationships that boys tended to become jealous of and competitive with their fathers, and girls to have similar attitudes toward their mothers. Because these feelings are socially unacceptable, children soon learn to conceal them. They get buried so deep in the unconscious that young people mature totally unaware they exist. These repressed emotions are expressed by most people in harmless behavior. But they could provoke an unstable, psychotic person into destructive acts.

Lizzie's accusers say the property deals inflamed her latent jealousy of Abby, and made her furious with her father. But given that Lizzie's mind has been read accurately, one has to ask: Jealous and angry enough to murder?

Those who believe her guilty also produced the theory that when Andrew went upstairs, he discovered his wife's body, then came down and accused Lizzie of murdering her, and Lizzie had to silence him. But is it likely that even so impassive and emotionally granitelike a man would not have been shaken by the sight of murder and cried out? Would he have accused Lizzie while he was spread out on the couch? That's where Bridget swore she saw him alive when she went up to the attic.

Bridget had rested in her garret for about half an hour when she heard Lizzie scream, "Murder! Help! Father has been murdered!"

What happened during that half hour? Bridget could only tell the court that she ran down the stairs to find Lizzie staring in horror at the battered corpse of her father. Lizzie was to explain that she'd been out in the barn during

140

The position of Andrew Borden's body when found, stretched out on the sofa.

the thirty minutes, looking for a fishing sinker. When she returned she had found Andrew killed.

From then on there was hysteria, and a confusion of comings and goings and a welter of conflicting statements from which the jury was to try to sort out the truth. Lizzie sent Bridget for a doctor. A neighbor who responded to Lizzie's screams said Lizzie was distraught and had volunteered that her mother had gone out and she didn't know where she was, but maybe she'd been killed too. Lizzie altered her story when she told it to Dr. Bowen and the police who arrived in quick succession. She said Abby had gone out, but now she added vaguely that maybe she had returned.

Dr. Bowen and the police officers examined the body and came to the conclusion that Borden had been killed by a sharp wedge-shaped instrument, like a hatchet. Bowen offered his opinion that the victim had died instantly; any one of the numerous blows would have been enough to kill him. The police were puzzled by Abby's absence, knowing how rarely she went out. Then, horror was added to horror. Bridget, trying to find something to do to blot out the dreadful sight downstairs, went up to dust in the guest room and came on Abby hacked to death.

As the news spread through the town, the inevitable crowd of the morbid, always attracted by murder and disaster, gathered outside the house. It was coming on to noon, and John Morse appeared to take his dinner with the Bordens. Because Morse was an outsider who looked like a tramp, and a known conniver in Borden's schemes, the crowd concluded he was not beyond murder if there was profit in it. The police had to protect him from the mob. But they held him for questioning and found that he had an alibi for Andrew's murder, though not for Abby's. Since they believed the crimes were the work of one person, they cleared him and he made himself scarce.

At the beginning, the police assumed the murders were the work of an intruder. But when the doctor established that Abby had been killed some two hours before her husband, they couldn't understand where the murderer could possibly have been during the interval.

They looked for the hatchet-shaped murder weapon. Bridget turned up several axe heads from the cellar. Marshall John Fleet, who came to head the inquiry, found one of Bridget's offerings interesting. It was an axe head with a freshly broken-off handle. There was no trace of blood on it. Fleet reasoned that a steel axe head can be washed clean. But not a wood handle. Perhaps that was why the axe handle had been broken off. The missing handle could not be found. Later on it was conjectured that Lizzie had burned it.

But this early in the proceedings Lizzie was not remotely suspected, although her story had some holes in it. One of the policemen had gone out to the barn and had reported to Fleet that it was hotter than the hinges of hell, and he couldn't stay in it for more than a few minutes. So how could Lizzie have been there for half an hour? And more peculiar still was that the dust in the barn lay thick and showed no sign of having been disturbed.

However, the next day, when Dr. Bowen told Fleet about Abby's poisoning, and the police learned from druggist Eli Bence that Lizzie, without a prescription, had tried to buy ten cents' worth of prussic acid to clean her fur cape, they turned their attention to her. It began to make sense. For one thing, she would inherit half Andrew's estate. Emma, who was away from home during the murders, was never suspected.

It required courage for the police to suspect one of Fall River's wealthy citizens. They would much rather have picked on Bridget, an Irish immigrant nobody. But Lizzie, to her own peril, made it clear that Bridget couldn't possibly have killed Abby, and had no earthly reason to do away with Andrew.

Lizzie was the most promising candidate—in fact, the only lead the authorities had—and they devoted themselves exclusively to nailing her. Since the axe had spilled so much blood, it stood to reason that the killer's clothes would bear the stains of the crime. The police searched the house for a bloodstained garment. They found none. A second, more thorough search also failed. Though it must certainly have been clear to Lizzie that she was the only suspect, she did not object when the police asked her, politely of course, for her shoes, stockings, undergarments and wool dress. These, as well as the axe head, were sent to the Harvard medical experts for microscopic examination.

On the advice of the family lawyer, Andrew J. Jennings, the sisters offered a five-thousand-dollar reward for the murderer. No one appeared with any information. The local newspapers, without mentioning Lizzie by name, implied she was the logical suspect. And when the public read that Andrew Borden had died without leaving a will, so that Lizzie and Emma would inherit a vast sum of money—well, there was a sufficient motive for murder.

Several thousand uninvited citizens gathered at the cemetery for the final rites. But those who had come to look at the conscience-striken face of guilt were disappointed. Lizzie was composed, impassive, pale in her weeds, showing nothing but the emotional restraint proper to native New

England mourners. It could have been any funeral, except that just as the coffins were about to be lowered into the graves, the police halted the service. The interment would be indefinitely delayed—an autopsy had been ordered. This dramatic turn of events made the whole occasion worthwhile for the home folks who now had something to talk about.

During the week after the murders, there was a constant stream of visitors to the Borden house. Mostly they were Lizzie's friends, acquaintances, good-works associates. They came to offer their condolences, along with the ritual calf's foot jellies, cakes, and other homemade dainties. In effect they were rallying round Lizzie, acting, so to speak, as character witnesses in her defense against the hints and innuendos of the press. However, their good intentions were to be used against Lizzie, for when it was announced that the inquest into the murders was to be held in private, the papers suggested that it was a cover-up by Lizzie's rich and influential peers.

It is difficult to say just how much effect this stirring up of sentiment would have had on the outcome of the inquest if Lizzie had been a good witness in her own behalf. The fact is that subjected to intensive questioning, Lizzie gave confusing and contradictory answers. Yes, she knew Abby had gone out. No, she only thought so. She had been in the barn. No, in the hayloft. She had found the sinker. She hadn't found it. She was out of the house for twenty minutes at least. She wasn't sure how long. And so on.

Unquestionably, Lizzie's performance on the stand did not prove her innocence. This, in the opinion of her de-

Lizzie Borden.

fenders, is what she would have had to do in order to be exonerated. There was still no hard evidence against her. One could reasonably expect that the coroner's finding would have been "Murder by person or persons as yet unknown." And further investigation by the police would have been ordered. A decision of this sort would not have cleared Lizzie, but it might have led the police to at least consider other possible suspects, however remote. They never did, for the inquest charged Lizzie with suspicion of murdering her parents and remanded her to prison, pending arraignment and pre-trial legal proceedings.

What a humdinger of a story it made for the newspapers! Not only the most horrendous of crimes, but the accused was a woman, and an heiress. And throw in that she was a pillar of the church, and add that she was active in worthy causes—well, reporters from all over country took off for Fall River.

One of them came up with a scoop during the nine months Lizzie was in prison. He wormed out of prison matron Regan the details of a conversation she claimed to have overheard between Lizzie and Emma. During one of Emma's daily visits the sisters had got into an argument. According to Mrs. Regan, Lizzie screamed at Emma, "You are giving me away!" Mrs. Regan was not called by the State to swear to this statement until the trial.

The testimony of druggist Eli Bence strongly influenced the outcome of the arraignment. His straightforward account of Lizzie's vain attempt to buy poison added an additional horrifying dimension to Lizzie's character. The implications were obvious. She must have or may have found a less ethical pharmacist whom she would persuade to sell her the ten cents' worth of prussic acid. And because the police had not been able to find any such vendor, there was a fallback assumption that she probably got it somehow, and sprinkled Abby's food with it. Once these assumptions were accepted, there was an answer to the question: "How come everybody who ate the same dinner the day before the murders got sick?" That was probably a cunning attempt by the accused to shield herself. Abby got the lethal dose, the others only enough to make it seem like summer complaint.

This structure lacked only the connecting mortar of fact. But legends need more than prosaic reality to build on. We create them out of our brightest dreams and darkest fears. And built high upon Bence's account was the terrifying image of a daughter who killed her parents, not in a frenzy of uncontrollable rage—but with cold, calculated, premeditated intent.

When the representatives of the Harvard medicos took the stand they reported their laboratory tests had revealed no traces of blood on the axe head, nor on Lizzie's shoes, stockings, wool dress, or any other clothing except for a red speck on an underskirt. Under oath, Lizzie attributed it to a flea—a not uncommon inhabitant of even the most splendid Fall River homes of the day.

Jennings, Lizzie's lawyer, placed great emphasis on the gory nature of the crime. The ferocity of the attack must have splashed the killer's clothes with blood. He stressed that despite the most thorough search by the police—on two separate occasions—no stained garment of any kind had been found. Without such evidence, he contended, Lizzie could not be linked to the crime. Though his argument weighed in his client's favor, the court found that there was enough reason to hold Lizzie for the grand jury, and she was sent back to prison.

Public opinion, at best unstable, now began to tilt toward Lizzie. The papers found that many people believed she was being hounded and persecuted—was being made the scapegoat of police failure to find the real murderer. This change in attitude resulted in considerable part from the willingness of prominent individuals and groups to insist publicly on her innocence. Her pastor proclaimed his faith in Lizzie; her associates in the women's auxiliary of the YMCA prayed for her; the Women's Christian Temperance Union backed her; suffragists and members of the women's rights movement spoke and protested in her behalf. Lizzie was becoming a controversial cause.

The arguments, pro and con, heated up when the grand jury convened to decide whether to indict her. It was then for the first time that Alice Russell, Emma's friend, was called by the prosecution to testify. Miss Russell related what had occurred while she was visiting the sisters on Sunday morning, three days after the murder. Emma and she were chatting in the kitchen when Lizzie appeared with a dress, splotched with brown smears, that she proceeded to tear into shreds and burn in the kitchen stove. The witness said Lizzie had explained the stains were brown paint which she couldn't get off and which had made the dress useless.

The record did note that the burning of the dress took

place a day after the police for the second time had searched in vain for a bloodstained garment. All that seems to have meant to the jurymen was that Lizzie had outsmarted the police. But why, having so successfully hidden this damning evidence, she should have burned it in front of a witness is a question hard to answer. Whether they asked it of themselves is not known. But they considered the evidence offered by witnesses sufficiently incriminating to conclude that Lizzie Borden must stand trial for murder.

The case of the People vs. Lizzie Borden came to trial nine months after she was arrested. Pale from her long prison confinement, she stood before the three justices and the jury in the New Bedford courthouse to listen to the charge against her. Once again, she answered the question, "How do you plead?" with a firm, "Not guilty."

Appearing as the principal counsel for the defense was George Robinson, a renowned trial lawyer from Boston. The prosecution was represented by a team headed by Hosea Knowlton, noted for its record of convictions. In terms of skill and ability opposing counsel were well matched.

The prosecutors could be confident, on the basis of testimony given at the previous hearings, that they had evidence enough to condemn the accused. But they ran into a snag at the outset when they tried to introduce the fumbling, contradictory statements she had made at the inquest. Defense counsel objected, pointing out that Lizzie had been under arrest and had not been informed of her right not to testify. The objection was sustained by the court.

Three doctors from Harvard, put on the stand in turn by the prosecution, testified that even the deepest of the blows that mutilated the victims could have been made by a woman. But the State's claim that the axe head was the murder weapon became questionable when cross examination elicited from the experts the opinion that not all of the cuts could have been made by the axe.

The prosecution's case was further shaken when Lizzie's counsel cross-questioned the doctor about the blood spot found on her underskirt. The Harvard laboratory tests had disclosed that it was not human blood; this helped substantiate Lizzie's flea explanation. The court upheld the defense objection to druggist Bence's poison story, on the ground that no connection had been proved between the poison and the murders. After ten days, having made substantially the same case that had brought Lizzie to trial, the prosecution rested.

A basic premise of the defense was that the police, unable to find the real criminal, were trying to frame Lizzie. Robinson undermined the credibility of the police witness who testified he'd gone into the barn and had found the dust undisturbed by producing two surprise witnesses. They were Tom Barlow and Everett Brown.

These Fall River teenagers related that they had visited the scene of the crime shortly after the news broke, to look for the murderer. Unable to gain entrance to the house, they had gone into the barn, where they'd searched high and low for clues. They could not have done so without leaving their footprints in the dust. The prosecution did its best to discredit the youngsters, but it couldn't budge them. The jury had to decide which of the two conflicting accounts to believe. If the boys were telling the truth, the policeman had lied—and that would strongly support the theory of a police frameup.

Seeking further support for the frameup theory, the defense called an itinerant ice cream vendor to the stand. This witness, an immigrant, testified in his broken English that he'd seen Lizzie go out to the barn as he was passing the house. The prosecution poked fun at his accent and got big laughs by bewildering him with rapid-fire questions, thus rendering his testimony practically worthless.

Critical to the outcome of the trial was the issue of the stained dress Lizzie had burned. Robinson approached this matter by first trying to establish that, contrary to the thrifty Fall River custom of keeping useless clothing in a rag bag, Lizzie discarded things she wasn't going to wear again. When the prosecution objection that this was irrelevant was sustained, Emma was called as a defense witness.

Of course, her statement was discounted in advance. Nobody expected her to testify against Lizzie. But she went further. She swore she had suggested to Lizzie that the old, paint-stained dress be burned. And she stuck to her story.

In his summation Robinson reviewed the totally circumstantial nature of the case against Lizzie. He reminded the members of the jury that to find Lizzie guilty they must agree with the prosecution that her motive for murder was a real estate dispute. They must not reasonably doubt that a woman of blameless character, a church worker, was suddenly transformed into an archfiend because her father had

The scene of the crime: the Borden home in Fall River.

transferred a piece of property to her mother—a piece of property worth only fifteen hundred dollars.

They must further believe that the axe head, which they had heard an acknowledged expert testify was identical with countless others made in the same factory, was the murder weapon—an assertion made by the prosecution, entirely without proof.

153

And finally, to find the defendant guilty they must convince themselves that she was, as the state claimed, at once a cunning criminal and a blundering idiot. Could they believe, with Mr. Knowlton, that the same person who was shrewd enough to conceal the incriminating evidence of the bloody dress from the police was also stupid enough to burn it in the presence of witnesses *while policemen were around and about the house?*

When Knowlton's turn came to sum up for the prosecution, he seemed to be advocating the feminist position—unpopular in the 1890s—as he told the all-male jury, "Women are no better and no worse than we are." His purpose, of course, was to counter the Victorian belief that a woman—the defendant specifically—was a delicate, fragile being, incapable of violence. Pursuing his theme, he cited instances of murders committed by women of impeccable reputation, some even church workers. He referred back to the medical testimony that the death blows could have been struck by a woman. And who else but this woman had the opportunity and the motive?

What was the motive? "Malice against Mrs. Borden inspired the assassin!" Abby Borden had no enemies but Lizzie. Why was Andrew Borden hacked to death? The jury should bear in mind that the Lizzie Borden who came down from the guest room in which she had left her stepmother dead was not Andrew Borden's loving daughter, but a murderess. It was in fear of retribution that she took the axe to him.

Why had Lizzie burned the bloodstained dress? Because she had no alternative. Because she knew that the police would search for it again, and it was safer to get rid of it at all costs, rather than run the risk of having this uncontrovertible evidence found.

As Knowlton concluded there was a stir in the courtroom while the justices conferred. The spectators argued in whispers about the outcome. Many wondered what the jury would make of the fact that Lizzie had not taken the stand in her own defense. Of course it was her constitutional right, but then wouldn't that be construed as an admission of guilt?

Silence fell as the chief judge began to speak. Before he instructed the jury, he said, he wanted to give the defendant an opportunity to speak. Lizzie rose slowly. "I am innocent," she said. That was all.

In his charge to the jury, the judge told them: "By seeking only the truth, you will lift this case above the range of passion and excited feeling, into the clear atmosphere of reason and law . . ."

The jury was out for only an hour. When they returned, having reached the legally required unanimous decision, Lizzie was told to stand to receive their judgment. The impassive composure she had maintained during her long ordeal was shattered by the foreman's "Not guilty." Lizzie broke into tears. The spectators cheered and applauded the verdict. The next day's newspapers celebrated the "victory of justice."

The sisters returned to Fall River where they bought an elaborate house which they lived in together for twelve years. Then Emma moved out because it seemed she felt that Lizzie and she should lead a retired life of mourning.

Lizzie would have none of that. Through the years she never made any attempt to seclude herself, as many in Fall River thought would be more proper for a person tried for murder. She gave parties and resumed her active social life. She was among the first in town to buy an automobile, in which she took daily drives. Fall River noted disapprovingly that she was always going to the theater in Boston and New York. In 1923, the sisters got into a dispute about some real estate. It resulted in a lawsuit which brought the Bordens back into the newspapers again. Emma dropped the case and retired into obscurity in New Hampshire.

Thirty-five years after her acquittal, Lizzie Borden, aged sixty-seven, died of natural causes in Fall River Hospital. Ten days later, Emma Borden died. The sisters lie in Fall River cemetery, in the family plot, beside their mother, father, and stepmother. Lizzie continued her good works after her death by leaving her money to an animal refuge.

Lizzie has not been allowed to rest in peace. The hope expressed in the court's charge to the jury has not been fulfilled. The case has not been lifted "above passion and excited feeling, into the clear atmosphere of reason and law." And it probably will never be.

ABOUT THE AUTHOR

LOUIS SOLOMON is a native of New York City, where he works as a television writer and producer. He received his bachelor's and master's degrees from City College of New York. Mr. Solomon has written for radio, the movies, and the theater. His varied background includes jobs as a teacher, truck driver, concrete curer, shoe salesman, and postal clerk. This is his seventh book for young readers.